Av

I

WITHIN 24 HOURS

Laurence Lameche

#1 Bestselling Author of
'HOW I BOUGHT 3 LONDON PROPERTIES FOR
A FOOTBALL TICKET'

Best wishes

Laurence Lameche

Copyright

Powerhouse Publications

Suite 124
94 London Road
Headington
Oxford
OX3 9FN

Cover design and formatting: Oxford Literary Consultancy
www.oxfordwriters.com

"Rags To Riches Story Began"

 **Chris, Spain**

"I'm very grateful to your dedication in helping people it has restored my faith in humanity."

The**Negotiator**

"His Example Will Inspire Other People"

 **Bharat, England**

"It is rare to meet people like you with your Approach, Ethics and Sincerity in helping people. The World needs many more Laurence Lameches."

FEMALE FIRST

"Winning Ticket To Success"

Dedication

Harrison this book is dedicated to you my son because you have always been Daddy's hero. You were born for the greater good of humanity. I believe in you and I will always be your number one fan. From the moment you were born and each year you get older, I have seen your greatness grow within you and now it is your time to shine, just like the star you were born to be. I love you more than you will ever know, now and for all eternity.

This book is also dedicated to You and to all the HEROES around the world who want to create the life of their dreams by awakening their inner hero within. You have greatness inside you and I wrote this book to help show you how to tap into your true potential.

Preface

I hope the ideas in this book change your life forever. Because they have helped me and thousands of other people just like you with families like yours from all over the world.

We only have limited time on this planet and I want you to live the life of your dreams by taking action today on creating the future you want tomorrow. Take the opportunity you have now because it is the best time to be alive.

This book has taken me a lifetime to learn and it is my way of passing it forward by writing down the ideas that I have learnt in these pages that have made such a difference in my life and in the lives of many successful people I know who have implemented these principles in their everyday lives.

You will learn easy-to-follow step-by-step processes to take back control of your life by changing the way you think, work and deal with different everyday situations that come along.

You are in safe hands because I wrote this book for you to awaken your own inner hero within 24 hours through these simple 24 chapters that will give you the secrets that you have been searching for. I am saving you the 20 to 30-year learning curve, and the pain and frustration I went through, to figure this out myself.

Don't put off reading the chapters inside this book for another day. Learn the lessons and put them into practice in your own life.

Always do your best because successful people do this whether they work for themselves or for someone else. Work as if your boss is watching you for every minute of every day.

The new habits you'll learn by taking small steps every day to improve your life will greatly benefit you in the long-term to create the life you've been dreaming about. So, it doesn't matter whether you are a young person in your first job, a business owner, employee, entrepreneur, investor or retired because you will find something within these pages that will help you in your life right now and take you to the next level.

Sometimes in life if you are feeling down and out and you're at the bottom, you've only got one way to go and that is to look up. Sometimes you just have to ignore the naysayers and believe in yourself, trust your own gut instincts and take risks. It doesn't matter where you've come from because all that matters is where you are going.

I failed at school: I didn't get any qualifications because I couldn't read and I was in the bottom classes. I was bullied at school and I didn't have any friends. So, I don't have a traditional education. I come from a single-parent family where my mother raised me and we were poor; my mother worked 3 jobs. I came to London and I slept in my car because I didn't have any money to pay for rent. I am self-made: I wasn't born with a silver spoon in my mouth. I come from the school of hard knocks. I know what it's like to have no money and to not have any food in the fridge.

I also don't like the sound of my own voice. I am an introvert by nature and I prefer my own company. I'm a bit of a loner, I am shy, I lack confidence and I don't have many friends but I am functional and I have learnt in life to sometimes get out of my own way and to make the moves to improve my life so that I keep moving forward and learning new skills along the way.

I learnt to become a visual and audible learner and I created easy-to-follow recipes for success. What made me want to write this book for you was to share with you what I have learnt in my life because it is much better to follow a recipe that works than spending years trying to figure everything out from the beginning or through trial and error.

I have recipes for you that will help you in this book make tiny shifts in your habits for years to come. I looked back on my life and figured out the habits I use that have got me to where I am today and I share this wisdom in this book.

The universal principles in this book will work for anyone and they aren't just based on my own personal journey.

I am very grateful that you chose to read this book and have read this far, so please don't stop now. Because most people will buy a book for the title and then just let it sit on the shelf, hoping that maybe the magic power of knowledge with action steps can transfer into their minds. Continue to read this book as I will make it as exciting and compelling as possible to give you the habits that will help you in your everyday life.

You will learn to replace your old habits with the new ones. It will be like changing an old battery for a new one. You don't need to add more time to your day, just replace the old habits with the new ones.

If you find this book helpful or valuable in anyway, I hope you give a copy to someone that you care about or recommend it. If you are a parent then please give a copy to your children, so they can learn how to awaken their own inner hero from within – this could be the greatest gift that you can give to any child or adult. I say this not to sell more books but to help empower as many people as possible around the world with this knowledge that they have the power to change their own lives. Sometimes it takes a lifetime to learn these secret habits and I only wish that someone would have written this book and given it to me many years ago! It would have saved me years of going through the pain of struggling to figure this all out by myself.

Life is short so why not do something you love. So much in life is not in our control but we can choose to control the thoughts that we think about most of the time which can either be inner peace or conflict, well-being or distress, happiness or unhappiness. The choice is yours to live life on your terms and to be happy in the garden of Eden in your mind or you can also embrace the chaos that the outside world often tries to infiltrate into our lives by distracting us, leaving us feeling out of control and following the masses.

What my hope for this book is to teach you that the only thing getting in your way, stopping you from achieving all your dreams, goals and happiness in life, is you. Transcend your own limitations and learn to get out of your own way.

Find your courage and just go for it. I hope you are inspired by this book to change your life for the better.

It pays to be brave, so if you are loving life doing things you feel you were born to do you are heading in the right direction.

Take the principles you will learn about to heart and, if not for yourself then do it for the people who love you, watching you and willing you to succeed in life behind the scenes.

I want to give you the tried and true results of what I have been doing for a long time. I want to empower you, not enable you with this knowledge. Empower you to take control of your life.

You are in the right place at the right time with someone that cares and I will hold your hand every step of the way, through these easy proven and transferrable processes.

I am giving you something that the world so desperately needs.

To learn the correct tools now will be better for you to take control of your life today so you can have a better tomorrow.

I believe the time is right to reveal what has been

hidden for so many centuries and bring this knowledge to public attention for the benefit of all.

Your life will change dramatically when your inner-hero-within habits become a new routine.

If you want to tap into your full potential and take control of your life, then this book can help you do that. So it doesn't matter where you are from or who you are, all that matters is that you are ready to begin right now in this moment and that you have an open mind and an open heart with a willingness to learn because your time has come to create a new way of being and to tap into your inner greatness.

The key to success is taking action. These principles work if you implement them to bring about fast improvements and the quicker you apply them in your own life, the more results you'll see – guaranteed. And remember that dreams come true if you have them!

Laurence Lameche
London, England
October 2020

CONTENTS

Awaken Your Inner Hero

An inner hero represents the best version of yourself to live life to your full potential. When you awaken your inner hero, the world of possibilities, opportunities and abundance will open up to you.

Remember that during your lifetime, you have to continue to battle and overcome your inner villain or defects just like a real-life superhero does in the movies. Just like Superman had his weakness, kryptonite (which was his vulnerability he had to overcome). So, you see all of us mere mortals also have the same challenges that we have to face in our own lives and in order to become what we were born to be, we need to awaken our own inner hero within.

In The Wizard of Oz, the Cowardly Lion wanted to meet the wizard to gain courage because he doubts himself, but he is in fact brave and he continues to do brave deeds. So, this was his inner villain that he had to overcome in his lifetime to awaken his inner hero from within.

In *Lord of The Rings*, Gandalf the Grey became Gandalf the White by overcoming his inner demon which was by fighting and defeating his enemy Balrog. So, when Gandalf says, "You shall not pass, go back to the shadow" is he really talking to his inner villain? He needed to overcome darkness in his life and by doing so he entered the light to awaken his own inner hero from within.

The inner villain will do everything in its power to fight against your growth and to knock your confidence, preventing you from developing and keeping you stuck in your old habits.

You must do all you can to defeat the villain and stay in control of your mind with the right thoughts, habits and actions to allow your inner hero to take over. This way, the villain loses and the hero wins just like in the movies.

The only way the villain wins is to remind you of your old disempowering story and to sabotage your subconscious mind along the way in life, so always be mindful of this happening. Let your hero take over to give you optimism and confidence and to create solutions to any problems that may arise.

However, the villain wants the opposite for you – robbing you of everything that is good and taking away your courage just like the lion in The Wizard of Oz or creating a demon to fight against you as in *The Lord Of*

The Rings. But say in your imagination that 'you shall not pass' and fight against it with the help of your inner hero who will win any battle that you have to face, to remain in control.

It is not about turning you from an introvert into an extrovert. It is about looking within to learn the simple skills today that will help you make the changes that will impact the rest of your life. There is no magic pill to take that will transform you overnight to manifest anything that you have ever wanted in your life. But with a little effort, it will be worthwhile, so don't stop believing.

This book isn't about just inspiring you with nice stories and motivating you as lots of other books do that. Instead it is about little actions that like a snowball rolling down a hill will gather momentum for you over time. By having the right state of mind and confidence, these are important factors for you to become a high achiever. Let the hero be in control of your life. Tap into your full potential and don't leave anything to chance.

Why are the hero and villain so different?

When people blame or think about whose fault it was they didn't get a promotion or pay rise, or why someone else got a disease, or why didn't a business work or why did a partner steal, they allow the villain to take over and be in charge. Whatever the small or big circumstance is, just accept it 'happened' and move on with life. Look forward to creating better outcomes and by doing this it changes everything.

The most dangerous enemy you have is the one that

lives within you.

Focus on solutions and not problems

Your inner hero is you living life to your fullest potential with nothing suppressing you anymore.

Do you want the old version of yourself to continue to control your life or do you want to unleash your new hero within? The inner hero is the real you that God wants you to be. You have limitless potential to utilise all the gifts that you were born with to become who you were meant to be.

It's all within you, no one else can make you change unless you want to. Let your inner hero take over your soul.

"A hero is an ordinary person who finds the courage, strength and determination to continue despite facing overwhelming obstacles."
– Laurence Lameche

The Story Of Two Wolves. Which Wolf Are You Feeding?

Would you like to learn about the most important battle that we face in our lives? It is a battle of good vs evil. Between our good thoughts and our bad thoughts. Which one wins? Well you get to decide for yourself!

A grandfather once taught his grandson a story about life, and told him that there are two wolves that live within each of us. *"A fight is going on inside me,"* he told *his grandson. "It is a terrible fight between two wolves. One of the wolves is evil — he is anger, regret, sorrow, greed, envy, arrogance, guilt, self-pity, resentment, lies, inferiority, false pride, superiority, and ego."*

He then continued, *"The other wolf is good – he is joy, hope, peace, love, kindness, serenity, humility, empathy, generosity, truth, compassion, and faith. The same fight is also going on inside you and inside every person."*

The grandson thought about what his grandfather told him and then he asked his grandfather, "Which wolf will win?"

His grandfather simply replied, "The one you feed."

This story is a powerful lesson because it reminds us that we are in control over our emotions and experiences.

In challenging situations it's easy to sometimes feel like a victim to the circumstances in our lives. To understand our feelings, experiences and negative thoughts, we often blame other people or events. Instead of looking from within ourselves, we look outwards to make sense of things happening to us in our lives. Why do we do this? Because it is our way of feeling more in control and coping with challenging situations.

This approach of dealing with these problems takes away from our own responsibility and freedom of choice. By blaming others for our own experiences, we feel more in control but this takes away our own power. We have lost in the moment that we depend on other people or things to feel a certain way. It doesn't matter whether the feeling is positive or negative because if we believe they are anything other than our own choice, we no longer take responsibility for our own experiences or emotions.

Having the freedom to choose which wolf to feed, you are making a life-changing decision. Do you feed the evil wolf who is your own worst enemy? The one who tells you all the bad things, negative thoughts to keep you suppressed. Do you really want to feed this wolf? Or are you already feeding him?

By not feeding this wolf – anger, regret, sorrow, greed, envy, arrogance, guilt, self-pity, resentment, lies, inferiority, false pride, superiority, and ego – you make a choice to instead use your energy on thoughts, emotions and feelings that help serve you in better ways. You no longer have to pay any attention to negative emotions when they occur within you by not giving them any focus or feeding them in any way. It may take time to learn, but what you will find is that this wolf will begin to lose its power and strength over you and it will surrender along with your unhelpful thoughts and emotions which will eventually drift away.

So, let's concentrate and feed the good wolf. It is important to remember that you have a choice to decide to feed the wolf with positive thoughts of *joy, hope, peace, love, kindness, serenity, humility, empathy, generosity, truth, compassion, and faith*.

Many of us look to external objects for our happiness. We think that these things (a relationship, a new job, a holiday, new clothes, a car, etc.) will make us feel a certain way. And while sometimes this brings us gratification, it won't last long term.

Happiness is a state of being. True lasting happiness comes from making a choice to be happy, rather than thinking that external things will make you happy. If you seek out happiness like a treasure you will find more of it.

You already have everything that you need to be happy right now with your thoughts. Finding happiness comes with feeding the wolf from within. When your wolf becomes bigger and stronger, you will find it easier to handle life's challenges. If you choose to only feed the good wolf, you will always win.

When there is no longer a battle within you, then you can listen to your inner voice for deeper knowledge and understanding that will guide you to choose what is right in every circumstance.

A man or a woman who has found peace within has everything. A man or a woman who is fighting a war from within has nothing.

How you choose to react to each wolf within you will determine your life. Starve one or you'll always be fighting an inner battle for the rest of your life. The choice is yours to decide, so which wolf do you choose to feed? Do you choose inner darkness or inner light?

This is such a powerful story because it applies to all our lives. We all have a bad wolf or a villain living inside us. But we also have a good wolf or a hero within us who is looking to be unleashed to the world. You are going to learn how to beat the villain and destroy it out of your life because once it is gone, you will be able to achieve so much more in your professional and personal life. Because there won't be anything holding you back to fulfil your true potential.

> *"Within us all there lives light (an inner hero) and darkness (an inner villain). The one you choose to listen to will determine the quality of your life."*
> — Laurence Lameche

Changing A Light Bulb or Changing Your Life

You could be doing many other things apart from reading this book like watching the television or going on social media, or spending time with friends. But you can always do these things if you choose to. Sometimes to get ahead in life you may need to sacrifice things – so what are you going to do, change a light bulb or perhaps change your life?

Awakening your inner hero within isn't about taking a magic pill that lets you manifest all your dreams and gets rid of all your problems while you do nothing. Don't wait for

someone to do something for you. It's about changing your thoughts and habits today.

Successful people do things that unsuccessful people don't want to do. Where are you going in life? So many people seem to struggle with this question.

When the vision of your life is clear, you'll stop wasting time on things not serving your goals and dreams. Your hours will be spent on achieving your goals. This way, procrastination will not wait until tomorrow. The habits taught in this book from my own trial and error and learning from other successful people will show you a new vision and you will feel like you have just been given a new pair of glasses.

This book is designed to give you the techniques, tools and habits to accomplish the 'how.'

What is your "Why"?

"There are two important days in our lives: the day that we are born and also the day we find out WHY." – Laurence Lameche

I don't consider myself to have skill or talent because they are not transferable, but technique is. So, in this book is an easy and transferable process that I'm going to share with you to help you to awaken your inner hero and to become the best version of yourself. Because I make things simple and easy to understand, anyone can do it and this is my way of passing it forward to share this knowledge with you through these pages.

When I was a little boy my parents got divorced and my mother decided all of a sudden to uproot and move, I would never have a say in the matter and I would always feel this was out of my control. I would go to a new school, make friends and then we'd pick up and relocate again.

Years later, I figured out that this was my 'why'

because I don't want anyone to tell me where to live, dress, or where I can eat, what I can do with my time, how to function or how much money I can make. I want to be in control of my life to make the decisions I want to make that empower me to feel alive with joy and happiness. I do not want anybody to take that away from me. I had finally found my why and my mission was clear.

I remind myself of my 'why' when I think about quitting or have a tough day. I know there is no way that I could give up. I know that I am always in control of my life.

If you attach your 'why' to your actions, you become unstoppable. When you anchor your goals in your life to your heart and soul, it then becomes much more than a well-intentioned thought.

What is your 'Why'?

1. Why do you want your income to go to the next level?

2. Why do you want more happiness in your life, more abundance, more intimacy, more passion, or to lose weight?

3. Why do you want to quit your job? Or get a promotion?

4. Why do you want to start a company?

5. Why do you want your partner or parents to retire?

6. Why do you want to spend more time with your family?

Why is it that your why is so important? Fear slows our momentum by self-sabotaging us to not take action. So by figuring out how to overcome obstacles with having the right tools, systems and strategies to create lasting habits in our lives, we can achieve anything that our heart desires with the right foundations.

It will be a shame to look back on your life in 10 to 20 years' time and realise that every day is the same, and you don't want to miss out on what could have been. Because you'll never get these years back.

There is a hidden enemy inside all of us trying to sabotage us in our lives. It works against your goals. These inner villains could be the fear, self-doubt and worry that have been holding you back all your life. And that is why I have written this book to help show you how to overcome these inner demons to awaken your inner hero within and to live life on your terms.

I hope you'll find the lessons you learn in this book will stick to you like superglue for a long time. My aim is for you to look back in a few years' time and be proud of yourself for all that you have accomplished because you have grown into a greater version of yourself.

It is all going to come together soon. So, continue to read more chapters because your future is waiting for you.

My book is different and here's why

I am honoured that you are spending your valuable time with me and have put your trust in me by purchasing this book. It's important to know that I won't waste your time because I know how busy you are and you've got many choices in personal development, motivation and success. Here is how this book is different from the rest:

1. Everything that you'll learn inside this book is timeless.

2. The principles taught in this book will be as relevant in the future as they are today.

3. Nothing in this book is theory because I actually do it.

There are lots of authors who write books but don't actually do what they are teaching you inside the pages of their books. But the difference between me and my so-called competitors is that I actually do practise what I preach inside these pages and I use these secrets that I will be teaching you in my life.

Gratitude

"Develop a habit for being grateful and continue to count your blessings every day for all great things that come into your life." – Laurence Lameche

SECRET #1 to Awaken Your Inner Hero Within 24 Hours

First thing when you wake up each morning and just before you go to bed at night commit to thinking about what you are grateful for in your life right now. This powerful process will help you to manifest more good things into your life, so always focus on the good things that you have already and remember all the blessings you have to be thankful for in your life right now to attract more.

I have heard many people say this over the years, but never really paid too much attention to it in the past. Now, I take this wisdom very seriously.

Because there is nothing more important than to focus on being grateful as soon as you wake up every morning, lay in bed and think for a few minutes in your mind of all the blessings you have in your life whatever they may be, however small or big, because by focusing on them you will attract more of these good things into your life.

Also, just before you go to bed at night think about all the things you are grateful for today.

10 Simple Things To Be Grateful For When IT's Tough

1. A roof over my head, plus a warm home.
2. Water to drink.
3. I don't have to go hungry.
4. I enjoy the small, free pleasures of life.

5. Internet access.
6. My family and friends.
7. My health.
8. The kindness of people I've never met before.
9. The setbacks that have made me stronger.
10. I am alive.

Think of things that you could feel grateful for even when you may be going through challenging times.

Being grateful every day will help focus your mind on thinking good thoughts and giving thanks for them in your life.

Here are some of the things that you could think about.

Ask yourself:

- What Am I Grateful For In My Life Right Now?
- What Am I Happy About In My Life Right Now?
- What Am I Proud Of In My Life Right Now?
- What Successes Do I Have In My Life Right Now?
- Who Do I Love?

Focus on what you are grateful for in your life right now. Don't focus on what you don't like, only focus on what you do want in your life because more of that will come into your life. The more you focus on what you are grateful for, you will attract more of that into your life.

"I believe that love can truly save the world." – Laurence Lameche

 Awaken Your Inner Hero Within 24 Hours

1. Every morning and evening think of all the things that you are grateful for in your life right now.
2. Make a list and write down 10 things that you are grateful for.
3. Count your blessings every day to attract more good things into your life.
4. Remember to only focus on grateful thoughts of what you want to attract more of.

Affirmations

"Every day I am better and I'm growing richer, in every way." — Laurence Lameche

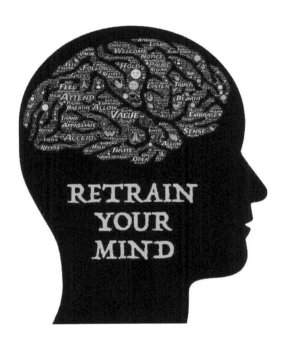

SECRET #2 to Awaken Your Inner Hero Within 24 Hours

Count your blessings every day to change your attitude and mindset to transform your life today into the one that you desire. The power of your words are so important, so count your blessings in your life every day through words of affirmation that will help you to improve the quality of your life with a healthy mind, body and spirit – it will change your reality.

When you wake up every morning listen to a 'Positive Affirmations' video on YouTube for thirty minutes while having breakfast. Instead of watching the television or the news or reading a newspaper or looking at social media, just make your breakfast and listen to affirmations. You can also do this while you are in the shower or having a bath as well.

You want to always fill your mind with good thoughts and good affirmations.

I remember years ago when I was a tour guide on the open-top buses in London, I really wanted to create an opportunity for myself to live and work in America. So every morning while I left my home walking to the nearest Tube station, or sometimes waiting for a bus, I would walk and say in my mind these words: *"Every day and every way I am getting better and better, and I am growing richer and richer in every area of my life."*

You need to almost re-programme your mind to let it absorb affirmations on a daily basis to fill up your mind with 'only good thoughts' every day.

You want to choose affirmations that will help you in your life that you can remember.

Here are some affirmations I have written for you to consider saying on a regular basis:

"I love myself, I love my life, I love my neighbour."

"I am a money magnet, wealth is attracted to me and I am growing richer and richer in every area of my life."

"I am wealthier, I am heathier and I am unstoppable."

"Every day and in every way I am getting better and better in all areas of my life."

"I am healthier, I look after my body and my body looks after me. I look and feel younger and I feel terrific."

"I am a born winner, I am a champion and I am the greatest."

"I am happy, I enjoy my life and I like myself because I have a good heart."

"I am kind and I am wonderful because I am me."

"I have great energy, love flows through me and people like to be around me."

"I love money and money loves me and we are all one big happy family."

"I am awakening my inner hero for the greater good of humanity."

"My soul is connected to my mind, body, heart and spirit and to all infinite intelligence."

"I was born to create a legacy so I can leave a dynasty."

"I am confident, I am powerful and I am a leader."

"I'm going to make it happen"

"I am clever, I am a genius and learning new things comes easy to me and I am very proud of myself for taking action every day to improve my life."

"I am a superstar and I am a superhero helping to improve the lives of many people around the world."

"I was born to win."
"I am a miracle."
"I get things done."
"I am a leader."
"I set a new standard."
"I do whatever it takes."
"I believe in my ability to figure things out."
"I get comfortable with the uncomfortable."
"I do what I say I'm going to do and I create my own luck."

"I am a millionaire."
"I am wise."
"I am living an abundant and great life."
"I am happy with who I am."
"I am confident, I am positive and I am powerful."
"I can do this."

To become a superhero, look from within. To see a superhero, look in the mirror and your reflection will show you. No one is you and that's your superpower!

Write a new chapter in your life, to make a difference to change the world.

Raise the spirit of your inner hero to overcome your

inner villain by constantly re-enforcing positive words of affirmations every day and if you catch yourself saying something that is not in your greater good then simply stop, pause and change those words, thoughts and actions to rephrase those things because your voice is your superpower.

Most people speak death during their lifetime. Your words are powerful. The Kingdom of Heaven is already inside of you. So, learn to live today and every day as if you are already in heaven, imagine a state of well-being, peace, joy, love and happiness and living a lifestyle full of abundance in every way possible.

Watch successful people and do what they do. Successful people invest in themselves – poor people they don't do that, they spend their money on entertainment.

Use A Power Phrase

Create a power phrase that you can use to help you in situations to overcome or accomplish something meaningful by igniting your inner hero from within like this one, "I command my subconscious mind to use my inner power, unique ability, to transform the lives of many people around the world."

What can you say to battle against your inner villain when it arises to keep you playing small or weak? What phrase can you say to help your inner hero fight back? Maybe it could be something like, *"I am a winner and I can do this"* or perhaps something like, *"My family needs me to succeed, so I will not give up."* Keep these phrases active in your mind to use at any time you may need them.

Write down some inner hero power phrases now. What could you say when you have to give a speech? Or walk into an important meeting with confidence? Or before you go out on a date? Or maybe there is a difficult subject you need to speak about to your partner or kids? Is there a phrase you can use to talk to your boss or employees?

Pick a power phrase and then practise saying it out loud over and over again in private. Really feel these words when you say them with energy and notice your state of mind change when your inner hero takes control.

Your confidence and state of mind are really important to the success, wealth and happiness you'll enjoy. All the millionaires and billionaires I have met are happy and successful people who have a unique ability to change their state of mind in a heart-beat. They all have an empowering story and a vision of where they are going. They let their inner hero take control to run their lives rather than allowing the dream-stealing villain to take control. Now you too have the tools and techniques to take control of your destiny.

Take this opportunity to be in control of your life and allow your inner hero to shine, it takes practice, strength and courage to take action. It may not happen overnight – just like going to the gym once or twice and expecting to have a six pack. However, if you want a six pack then you can always go to the supermarket and buy one! But in all seriousness, like anything worthwhile in life, it takes work and commitment to create new habits and routines that will make a difference to help you to achieve the success your inner hero wants for you.

"Do one thing each day that will take you one step closer to your goal." – Laurence Lameche

---

 Awaken Your Inner Hero Within 24 Hours

1. Listen to YouTube videos of affirmations every morning when you wake up
2. Write a list of your favourite affirmations
3. Remember to say these affirmations to yourself on a regular basis when you are walking, going out, on the train, bus, car, in the shower or at the supermarket. Practise, think and remind yourself about all the good sayings you have developed to help you though out the day.

Read

*"Get started **Today. Tomorrow** can wait."*
– Laurence Lameche

SECRET #3 to Awaken Your Inner Hero Within 24 Hours

Constant learning, reading and self-development is the answer to improving your life for the better, staying ahead of your competitors and continuing to grow. This will allow you to tap into the wisdom of other great minds that have lived and learn the tools and secrets to help you become happier, healthier, more successful, fulfilled, have peace of mind, be in a loving relationship, to find joy and confidence. Read a book a day to keep the villain at bay and help to awaken your inner hero within.

Read for between 15 to 60 minutes every day about what it is you want to do, become or have in your life. The average person only reads four books a year, but if you can, read one book a month in a particular area that you want to focus on.

Within 5 years you will be among the top 5% experts in the world in that particular field. If you decide to master one area that you love, you will always be in control of your own destiny. And you will become so unstoppable, that none of your competitors will be able to catch up with you. So read about your specialised subject.

Bill Gates says he reads 50 books a year.

Elon Musk reads 2 books a day.

Warren Buffet reads 500 pages a day.

27% of the general population reads nothing.

Successful CEOs read, on average, 60 books per year or 5 books per month.

Push yourself to greatness. And commit to continuous learning.

Put aside time each day to read and set yourself a goal to read for at least 15 to 60 minutes a day. Or to read one chapter a day.

If you find reading challenging, then start to listen to audio books every day to consume as much as possible. Not all books are made in audio but it is worth choosing which ones are and then dedicating some time each day or each week that you listen to audios so that you can continue to learn and grow.

You want to create a routine that works best for you and for your lifestyle and if you are not able to do this daily then take time to read over the weekend.

I personally find it better to implement reading when I first wake up in the morning and I look at a new book that I am reading and I look at the number of pages. Then, when I start to read it, I can see how many hours it will take me to complete the book because I am a slow reader. I like to take my time to remember the content and the most important things I am reading about I like to highlight or underline that section so I can come back to that book any time and flick through the important points again. It is worth doing this, but at first, I never wanted to mark my books in any way. However, now I feel this is essential because if I don't do this then I may forget which books I have read or not read on my bookshelf!

The reason why I like to read in the morning is

because it sets you up for the day and it gets you to focus on important things like learning something new rather than wasting time looking at the television or going on social media that just distracts you and this is what happens for the rest of the day.

We have so little time on this planet that we need to make the most of it.

Become a reader and commit to becoming an expert in your field by reading books by other experts in your industry and continue to learn something new every day.

Spend 5 Hours A Week On Deliberate Learning

The 5-hour rule involves spending five hours a week, or one hour each working day, focused on deliberate learning. This means setting aside time to give your full attention to learning and development, without getting distracted by other work.

"Yesterday I thought that changing the world was smart. But today I realise that changing myself makes me clever." – Laurence Lameche

Awaken Your Inner Hero Within 24 Hours

1. Read between 15 to 60 minutes every day in the morning or listen to audio books.
2. Successful CEO's read on average 60 books per year, so 5 books a month.
3. Continue to learn, grow and develop your mind by spending 5 hours a week to focus on your chosen subject so that you can be in the top of your chosen field.

Listen To Motivational Talks and Watch Videos

"If you want to fly with eagles then don't waste time with turkeys, (unless it's Christmas or Thanksgiving!)" – Laurence Lameche

SECRET #4 to Awaken Your Inner Hero Within 24 Hours

Become inspired every day with positivity flowing into your mind, and hope in your heart, when you listen to motivational talks that inspire you, uplift you and encourage you to live life on your terms. Take action today on following your dreams to create the future you desire tomorrow.

Listening to a motivational speaker can help to inspire you to look from within and tap into your hidden inner potential for a better life.

You could listen to motivational videos on YouTube, talks, audios or podcasts. The best time to do this would be in the morning as soon as you wake up and get ready for the day ahead. Or listen to them on your way to work in the car, bus or train and also listen to them during your lunch break and on your journey back home.

I enjoy listening to motivational videos in the morning as soon as I wake up and make breakfast because I want to fill my mind with good things at the start of my day so I am in the right frame of mind to take on the world for the rest of the day.

I remember one motivational speaker called Les Brown who said something along the lines of *"The richest place on earth is the graveyard, because it is here you find all the dreams and hopes that were never fulfilled, the books that weren't written, the songs that never got sung, the inventions that never happened, the cures that didn't get discovered, all because those people were too afraid to take action to carry out their dream."*

Use daily motivation to feed your mind along with your body. Listen to inspirational thought leaders on YouTube. Feed positive information and energy into your brain every day to remind yourself what your goals are. If you are going to think, then you might as well think big positive thoughts on how you will get there. Focus on one thing at a time. Work on your habits every day, one at a time.

"The law of attraction is visualising what you want, believing it's possible and taking action to get it."
— Laurence Lameche

Awaken Your Inner Hero Within 24 Hours

1. Listen to motivational speakers to help inspire you on YouTube, TED talks, audios and podcasts.
2. Listen to motivational speakers while making breakfast, going to work, at lunchtime, leaving work or in the bathroom while having a bath or shower.
3. Feed your mind with daily motivation to get in the right frame of mind to create a better world within.

No Social Media When You Wake Up In The Morning

"Don't waste your time on social media watching somebody else's life – go out and live your own."
– Laurence Lameche

SECRET #5 to Awaken Your Inner Hero Within 24 Hours

Each day you wake up in the morning with a smile on your face is a golden opportunity to finish what you were unable to do yesterday. It's really important to make the first hour of every new day count because it will set you up for success for the rest of the day. So, take positive action because today will never happen again, so don't waste it as you were born to succeed.

It is one of the most addictive things you can do and it will potentially unbalance your day if you reach for your phone to see how many messages, emails, likes and comments to your posts you have gotten first thing in the morning and this leads to stress and anxiety.

This gives you no peace to start your day calmly. So, stop checking your smartphone as soon as you wake up in the morning, so that you can relax your mind.

Also, turn off alerts as this is really distracting throughout the day and it only interrupts your focus and work.

You also may find it a good idea to not take your phone to the toilet with you because you could waste a lot of time looking on social media, watching videos and this time could be better spent working on your dreams instead. Remember to not flush away your dreams in the toilet!

One of the best things you can do every morning is to resist the urge to look at technology as soon as you wake up. Leave the television, radio and cell phone off. And only turn your computer on when you have organised and planned your day.

Most people are glued to their smartphones which can be a source of stress and distraction in our lives if not controlled. Even though they were designed to help us. People are so addicted to their smartphones that about 80% of us check them within the first 15 minutes of waking up every morning.

When you wake up to check your phone, your attention and time are being hijacked by checking social media, emails or messages. You are allowing other people's opinions into your mind, which in turn pollutes your thinking, ideas and focus.

Focus your attention on your own goals. Imagine letting hundreds of people into your own home first thing in the morning when you wake up, allowing them to shout their opinions and requests at you. You wouldn't do it, so don't let them into your mind through your phone!

Improve yourself in the morning by working on your goals and preparing for a successful day. Your ability to focus is decreased when you start the day glued to your smartphone. The inner villain is at work to stop you focusing throughout the day because when you check social media or emails, your brain releases a lot of dopamine, and this neurochemical makes you feel rewarded. Just like children crave sweets, so does the brain crave dopamine. So, if you start your day scrolling through social media or emails, then your brain will stimulate you to keep repeating this behaviour all day because it knows that it will quickly feel good. So, fight this inner villain against the cravings of your brain. To win this battle, all you have to do is not check your smartphone after you wake up so that you can be calm and relaxed and remain in control.

If you are a parent, you could help your children by taking away their phones for the first hour when they wake up (this could be a fun game to play). Or ask your family, partner, house mates, wife or husband to hide your phone for the first hour of each day or perhaps with permission change each other's passwords so for the first hour they can't get into their phone.

Do whatever it takes to come up with ideas to stop yourself from looking at social media when you wake up for the first hour each day and notice the addiction to social media will start to drift away; it may be challenging at first but with practice and over time it gets easier. So, start to implement this habit as quickly as possible for a better life.

Two Ways To Stop Checking Smartphones In The Morning

1. Before you go to sleep, put your phone on flight mode, so you don't notice new messages or notifications.

2. Have other morning habits planned out already instead of checking your phone. Make a list of what else you could be doing with your time just like:
    *   Reading.
    *   What are you grateful for in your life right now?
    *   Listening to Affirmations.

- Working on your Goals.
- Exercising.
- Listening to Motivational Talks or a Podcast.
- Spending quality time with your kids, partner or family.
- Scheduling your day.
- Prioritizing your tasks.
- Making a healthy breakfast.

Every morning, choose one or more of these activities instead of checking your phone.

Starting your day like this will allow you to feel more in control and relaxed. You will feel less stressed and be more focused and productive during your day.

Do It Now

Change only happens when you take action, so I encourage you to avoid using your smartphone and follow these tips for the first 60 minutes of your day. The way you start your day will set the tone for the rest of your day, so start it well.

"Inside of you is the hero you've been looking for."
— Laurence Lameche

 Awaken Your Inner Hero Within 24 Hours

1. Ban social media for at least the first hour when you wake up in the morning.
2. Turn off alerts, notifications and put your phone on silent when you are working on something important, otherwise you will always be interrupted throughout the day and you will lose focus.
3. Do not flush away your dreams down the toilet by taking your phone with you and wasting time on unsocial media.

Turn Off The News
To Make You Smarter No News Is
Good News

"Wrong information is riskier than ignorance, so be careful." – Laurence Lameche

SECRET #6 to Awaken Your Inner Hero Within 24 Hours

Do more today and every day than what you are getting paid for. This secret to success in being able to do this in everything that you do will help you in your life. So, make yourself so valuable that you become an essential part of the company. Go the extra mile – it'll be worth it.

You may be thinking, 'Oh Laurence, come on, this is common sense.' But common sense is not always common. By not listening to the news or reading about it, will do you the world of good. Because when you think about it, all the news is the same, it's always bad so why would you want to fill your mind with negative and unpleasant things, so turn it off.

Because you have to ask yourself this question, 'How does watching the news make you feel?' If it doesn't make you feel good, then don't watch it. Now, some people will say it's good to keep up with world news and what is happening in the world – but why? I feel it is far better to not allow negative thoughts to come into your mind. Why would you want to feel angry, upset and worry about what you see, hear and read about on a daily basis.

Bad news sells, so why watch the negativity and disturb your mind and peace. Also cut down on watching television and do something that will enhance the quality of your life like spending time with your family, reading, exercising and eating healthy food. It is not in your best interest to watch television because it is called a program for a reason. And why do you think they call it a remote control? Be mindful of the hidden messages out there.

A success-robbing villain to watch out for is watching, listening to, or reading the news. If you think about it, we grow up getting nothing but negative news put into our minds, every day. If you think about it, the news is about economic crisis, sickness, suffering, scarcity, disasters, terrorist attacks, wars and murders. Our brains are constantly bombarded with this information.

It is difficult to focus on positive thoughts when the majority of daily data we consume is completely negative, when we get information about a world which seems doomed. Even if you are a really positive person by nature, then this constant bad news will start to slowly affect you in a negative way.

Because the negativity overpowers the positive thinking part of our brains. Research done by UCLA found that the average person has around 70,000 thoughts every day. And 80 percent of these thoughts are negative, with the majority of these thoughts flooding into our minds the next day. And so, consuming negative news is a leading cause to this statistic.

This will affect you whether you like it or not because we get the news online, television, newspapers, radio, social media, apps and phones. Our subconscious mind takes it all in whether we want it or not. So, your inner villain is getting stronger with all this negativity. Because it encourages thoughts like, 'Why do you think love will work for you when famous celebrities are getting divorced? The economy is crashing, so why set up your own business now? The world is more obese now so why get in shape?' The negative news slowly chips away at your confidence over time when you consciously or subconsciously absorb even a little of it. Rather than to motivate you to follow your dreams, you get stuck and stay where you are, losing control of your life and following the masses.

To defeat this villain, do yourself a favour and go on a 30-day news diet, where no news equals good news, so to speak. This means don't watch the news, read about it or listen to it in any way. And don't ask your friends, family or dog about it because you'll be barking up the wrong tree if you do!

Instead, use this time to focus your energy and search within yourself to work on developing what you are learning about in this book — to continue to grow into the best version of yourself you can become. Spend time with loved ones, go into nature, read books that inspire you and think about creating an action plan to start on working towards your goals. Gain confidence by believing in yourself and taking action.

Spend time on yourself instead of wasting it on the news. Remember, it's not only the time you lose by watching or reading the news that you will never get back, but also the damaging after-effects that do the most harm.

So, commit to yourself in this moment to take the 30-day news diet challenge. Then, write down a list of things that you will do to occupy your time instead. Think about what you have been putting off in your life or what you would like to be doing like exercising, eating healthy food, gaining specialised knowledge by reading in your chosen field, writing a book, learning a new skill by taking an online training. Create a business plan, will you spend more quality time with your kids, partner, parents or friends?

Whatever you choose to do, this news cleanse will do you the world of good, while gaining more time each day doing things that you enjoy and allowing you to escape the negativity to move forward in the right positive direction. Do you know how much time you waste by watching television? By doing this you are not focusing on working towards your goals. On average, we spend 4 hours a day watching television. Turn off the news – it could be one of the best decisions you've ever made.

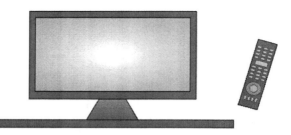

*"There is a monster in your home called a television.
It's an electronic mind-altering device and it's called
a PROGRAM and a remote CONTROL for a
reason. It's designed to psychologically change your
views on reality."* – Anonymous

 Awaken Your Inner Hero Within 24 Hours

1. Turn off the news and see how much more positive your life will be.

2. There is nothing good about reading, watching or listening to the news – it only harms your mental well-being with all the negativity that gets into your mind.

3. If you want to find peace in the world, turn off the news and you'll soon find inner peace instead of internal war. Don't pollute your mind with watching economic crisis and instead work on your dreams to monetise them. Ignore sickness, suffering and disasters – instead fill your mind with healthy thoughts like hope, joy, happiness and practise gratitude, affirmations. Listen to motivational talks and audio books.

4. Take a 30-day news diet, where you turn off the news to take back control of your life.

Don't Let Other People Affect Your Mood

"A Lion Doesn't Lose Sleep Over The Opinion Of Sheep." … Baa, Baa …

SECRET #7 to Awaken Your Inner Hero Within 24 Hours

Never let anyone spoil your day. I know it's easier said than done, right. Nothing external has any power over you unless you let it. Your time is too valuable to waste your days fighting the mental strain of hate, envy and jealousy. So, protect yourself carefully.

You are in control of your own destiny, so don't let other people's attitude of doom and gloom affect how you feel about yourself. You are very special, so don't allow others to take away your power in any given moment.

Be selective about the people that call you because you have to understand certain people want to either gossip, or they'll bring drama to your life, or they want something. So, protect your peace every day and distant yourself from negativity. I find it easier not to compare myself to others because I'm only in competition with myself; I just need to be me.

No One Can Hurt Your Feelings Unless You Let Them

Remember that you are in control of your emotions, so don't give up your power to allow others to control you this way. You are the person that is in control of your feelings and emotions. When you know where you are going in life, you will not let situations get in the way of your goals for long. When you set ambitious goals for yourself and you work hard to achieve them, you will soon realise that you won't have time to allow for things to upset you and to keep you from achieving your ultimate goals. Stop caring about what other people think of you.

Words

Do you remember the childhood saying, "Sticks and stones may break my bones, but words can never hurt me"? It is easier said than done, so you have to do your best to not let other people's words or actions affect you; the only way they can affect you is if you let them.

Don't let these negative words affect your emotions to change your mood to tears or stress you to make you ill. Or decide to live with inner peace where other people's words can no longer affect you.

How To Deal With Worry

Death: Accept it as a fact of life. It will one day happen to all of us, so what's the point of spending your life worrying about it?

Poverty: Do not worry about what you have in regards to wealth.

Fear of criticism: Don't worry about what other people think of you because their opinion doesn't matter.

Old Age: None of us are getting any younger, so just embrace it and don't see it as a handicap but as a blessing of wisdom that youth cannot understand.

Loss of Love: Get along without love. It's better to be single than in an unhappy relationship.

Destroy the thoughts of worry by deciding that 'nothing in life is worth worrying about.' If it's not a problem, then don't create one. When you decide this, you'll experience calmness of thought and peace of mind, which will bring you more happiness.

Worry: It Kills Quicker Than Work

Will Rogers once said that worry was similar to a rocking chair, you can be busy rocking but it won't get you anywhere. Nothing is solved by worrying, it only puts added pressure on you. It's best to anticipate problems before they come up and then develop alternative solutions for them.

If you have a problem that may branch out into different directions perhaps create a 'decision tree' and have a plan of action for each situation. A careful plan of action to each problem will help you to overcome your worry to the situation and will save you time in unnecessary worry.

Worry stops us from going from pain to pleasure. It stops you in your tracks and can keep you stuck for weeks, months, years or even longer. It can keep you trapped in a toxic relationship or from taking a good relationship to the next level. It stops you from leaving a job to starting a business that you've always dreamed about doing. It can also keep you stuck in self-destructive behaviours like gambling, drinking, or taking drugs.

"Worrying is thinking about something in your mind that you don't want."
— Laurence Lameche

Do Not React To The Situation

You can't control other people's behaviours towards you, but you do have control of your emotions so it's best not to react to the situation. Don't allow anyone to make you feel bad because there will always be people in the world who like upsetting other people whether they are friends, family, work colleagues, neighbours or strangers.

When you have to deal with such people understand that they are trying to upset you and it's not because you have done something wrong to them; it's because they have a problem with themselves. So, remind yourself 'it isn't about me', and instead don't allow this person to upset you because you are in control of your emotions and your life. Think of it as your inner villain wanting to get under your skin to annoy you, so ask yourself this question, 'How would my inner hero react?' And your inner hero would not react to let anyone else upset your inner peace and well-being.

Stress

Many people think that they have to wait for a better time because they have stress in their life right now.

When I teach people about getting into property investing with little money they think, "What if it doesn't work?", "What if my spouse doesn't agree with me doing this?", "What if I fail?" And many other worries and concerns.

Say, for example, you need to make some big changes in your life like switching careers or ending a toxic relationship but you worry about not finding someone new so you stay in the bad relationship out of fear, or with starting a new business you say to yourself, "What if I go broke?" Just imagine you do nothing and you have the same worries a year from now or 5 years from now. Nothing has changed and you are in the same place you are today. You don't take action and you are stuck. You are bored with your job, overweight and still having to wake up to the same toxic relationship every day.

Experience how you feel right now thinking about this because that is how you will continue to feel if you let worry control your life.

You are worth more, so don't let worry have a hold on your life anymore because this is the villain you need to overcome that hides within you. There is a better version of yourself waiting to break free of worry if you awaken the inner hero within.

I wasted years of my life because of worry. I worried about not being smart enough because I failed school with no qualifications; I worried about not being able to get a job or having any money; I worried about writing a book because I found it difficult to read and write. But then I ignored these stories I was telling myself and the worry just disappeared and I just took the leap of faith. One day, I thought, 'I am going to write my book by this deadline' and I took action and I just did it because I didn't want this inner villain to get the better of me with constant worry.

F.E.A.R. is an **acronym** for **False Evidence Appearing Real**. If there is no threat of physical danger, no threat of losing someone, there's actually nothing to **F.E.A.R.** at all because it is an illusion.

Fear Is A Costly Human Emotion

The enemies of success are fear, doubt and indecision. If you have fear and doubt, you will be indecisive and indecision turns into fear. It then turns into doubt. These enemies are so dangerous because they grow within us slowly, unnoticed.

Seven fears to be careful of that get in the way of success are: poverty, loss of love, criticism, ill health, old age, liberty and death. Because your mind works on transforming your thoughts into reality, you must do all you can to focus the power of your mind to eliminate negative thoughts and replace them with positive thoughts. If you can master your thoughts, you master your life by overcoming your fears.

If you experience setbacks, delays and temporary defeats, then hope gives you courage to continue until you have overcome the fears and doubts from time to time.

You have two choices: you can either decide to watch, wait, grow old and bitter or you can decide to choose to become an achiever who makes things happen with a positive outlook on life. The choice is yours to always make.

Fear of Failure

The biggest enemies we have that we must overcome are not a lack of opportunity or ability but fears of rejection and failure and doubts that we feel. To overcome your fears, you need to do the things you fear. Why let external events affect you and distract you? Learn from the Disney movie Frozen and just "Let It Go"!

"Most people spend their whole lives looking for 'the one', when the one has been waiting within to be found." – Laurence Lameche

Awaken Your Inner Hero Within 24 Hours

1. Don't let other people affect your mood or how you feel. Remember that no one can upset you unless you allow them too.

2. *Worry is like a rocking chair. You can be busy rocking but it won't get you anywhere.*

3. Take back your power and let nasty words roll off your back like water does to a duck. Quack, quack!

4. If someone upsets you, take a deep breath, relax and ask yourself this question: 'What would my inner hero do?' and don't let the person or situation get to you. Keep control of your emotions, remain calm and carry on being the hero you were born to be and do not let this inner villain take control by upsetting you.

5. FEAR is False Evidence Appearing Real so overcome this by feeling the fear and doing it anyway.

Happiness

"Let your spirit fly, your eyes shine and your heart beat by reading more pages in this book."
— Laurence Lameche

SECRET #8 to Awaken Your Inner Hero Within 24 Hours

Laugh at yourself and at life. When you learn to laugh, your worries will be a distant memory and this will help you in any situation to ease your mind and I have personally found that in the most testing of situations that life throws your way, a little laughter can help make you feel a whole lot better and it's sure better than crying.

Do what makes you happy by being yourself. Start valuing your true worth and move forward in the direction you choose to go.

If you are willing to follow your heart and tap into your full potential to be courageous to make a difference in this world while you are here, then you become unstoppable.

To make a change in any area of your life, start to write down a list of: 'What makes my heart smile?' When your actions are aligned with your heart, your confidence will build and the doubt dies.

Did you know that you'll live longer if you smile more and it lowers your blood pressure? It will improve your marriage and you'll make better friends.

Just imagine yourself standing up straight, your head held high and your shoulders back. When you talk with enthusiasm, positivity and energy you are fun to be around, with a smile on your face, and you radiate abundance everywhere you go.

When you become the person, you want to be you attract the right people who are similar into your life and you repel people who may bring you down. So, start to attract an abundant lifestyle by thinking and acting it with everything you do. You are a bright light in this world, so don't let others dim it.

You already have it, as it lies inside of you.

Happiness comes from within which is the opposite to what most people think. Because a lot of people think that happiness comes from material things like money, success, nice home, fast cars and luxury holidays. This is why a lot of people walk around depressed because they are searching for outer things to make them happy when happiness comes from within.

Start to think about what makes you happy? I think this is a really overlooked question because when we meet or speak to our friends and family, we don't tend to ask them or people we meet this question. What brings you joy, makes you laugh, and what makes you feel alive and makes your heart smile? What really makes you happy? Think of when you were a child – what things used to make you happy? What makes you smile? Is it spending time in nature, going to a concert or sporting event? Spending time with your children, family or partner? Do you enjoy walking barefoot on the sand at the beach?

It is important not to confuse happiness with goals. I have financial goals, material goals, and achievement goals. I just wanted to make sure that you understand the difference between these.

Write down a list of things that make you happy and activities that bring you joy and blessings to be grateful for.

So many people go through life looking forward for tomorrow or the weekend, next week, next month or a summer holiday or next year, instead of living in the present for today, right now. That is why it is so important to live in the now, so why not choose to be happy now?

Why not focus your thoughts on being happy right this second, and learn to live life in the moment, for the moment. You can decide to make this decision, it's your choice. Appreciate being alive and healthy today.

It is surprising how many people focus on what could go wrong in their life rather than focusing on what could go right. Concentrate on living a healthy and abundant long life. If you focus your energy on positive outcomes to get more wealth, health, happiness and abundance you will attract more of it into your life.

It is better for you to work in a job you love. What I have found is that taking jobs you don't like is not going to help you be happy. In fact, I had many jobs myself when I first moved to London to just get by to pay my rent, food, travel and expenses.

But I wasn't happy in any of those jobs because I didn't like any of them and what helped me is the last job I got fired from. Many years ago, I asked myself this question, 'What could I do for work that I would be excited to get out of bed each morning and I would actually enjoy my job?' So if you can ask yourself this question and think about what job you would enjoy, then look to change careers.

And if you are working, then when you get home spend some time on working on your dreams and goals in your spare time rather than watching television or going on social media or wasting time by not focusing on your goals. So, do what you love.

Smile More To Feel Better

When you smile, it makes you feel better and happy. Experts say a smile changes your body's chemistry and well-being.

When you smile, people notice that in your voice and will open up more to you in person or on the telephone as they can hear your smile in your voice. Keep a mirror near your phone so you can see yourself when you speak to people and remind yourself to smile.

Laugh At Yourself

Remember to laugh at yourself or your situation, so that you don't take yourself too seriously.

Learn good health habits. Have a healthy diet with plenty of exercise, eliminate substance abuse and unhealthy eating habits to create the lifestyle you want to live so that you can feel better about yourself both outside and within.

If your mind is healthy and strong, your body will benefit as a result. You do become what you think about.

Being Invited To Talk In A Hotel About My Book

I remember one time being invited to give a talk about my Amazon No.1 Best-Selling book called '*How I Bought 3 London Properties For A Football Ticket*' at a hotel.

A guy approached me and said, "Excuse me, are you Laurence Lameche?" I said, "Yes, I am." He said, "My girlfriend is a huge fan of yours and she loves your work."

He told me that he wanted to do something special for his girlfriend as it was her birthday next week. He bought a copy of my book and asked if I could autograph it for her because he said, "she will be thrilled to get a signed copy from you".

I said, "Yes, I'd be happy to sign it for her." Taking his pen, I wrote on the first page inside the book, *To Jane, with Love, Happy Birthday, Laurence Lameche.*

Then, he gave me a hug and thanked me. But as he was leaving, I asked him, "Is this going to be a surprise for Jane?" And he said, "Oh yes," smiling from ear to ear, "It certainly will be Sir, because she's expecting an engagement ring."

To find out more about the incredible gift that Jane received on this special day, that could potentially also change your life forever as well, go to:

www.PropertyBookSecrets.com

"True heroes find a way to help and serve others."
— Laurence Lameche

Awaken Your Inner Hero Within 24 Hours

1. Follow your heart and do things that make you happy.
2. We only have one life, this is not a rehearsal, so make every moment count to bring happiness into your life and enjoy every day and make the most of it.
3. If you want to live longer and feel better, smile more.
4. Find a job you love.
5. Laugh at yourself and don't take life too seriously.

Procrastination

"I once bought a book on procrastination, but I put off reading it for 2 years. Please don't make the same mistake as I did — read this chapter now!"
— Laurence Lameche

SECRET #9 to Awaken Your Inner Hero Within 24 Hours

Never again allow your mind to wonder on unimportant things. Your hours are precious so treasure them because the one thing we can never get back is time. As each day goes by you get older and you'll have less time to do the things you want to achieve. So when you dedicate yourself today by taking the right action now and not tomorrow, you will win.

Learn from other successful people and repeat the same things they do until you get the same results.

Concentrate on the most important task and do it well until you finish it. This is the key to achieving success and happiness in your life.

The most important decision you can make every day is to decide what you will do straight away and what to leave for later.

If you can develop a habit of starting and finishing important jobs, this is one of the keys to living a wonderful life and having a successful career and feeling good about yourself.

Do you remember the story of a man who stopped a stranger in London and asked: "How do you get to Wembley Stadium?" To which the stranger replied "Practise, practise, practise!"

To master any skill, you need to practise and it is said that if you want to be an expert in your field you will need to practise your chosen craft for 10,000 hours.

With practice you can learn any skill, behaviour or habit because your mind is a muscle that grows stronger with use.

The six P formula says, "Proper Prior Planning Prevents Poor Performance."

Time Management

The key to your success in work and life is your ability to control what you do next and to choose between what is important and unimportant. Discipline yourself to do the most important task first, whatever that maybe. You will get more done than the average person and you'll be much happier as well.

Ask yourself this question before starting anything: "Are there potential consequences for starting or not doing this task?" Think about your decisions, choices and behaviour in your work and personal life.

Think about the long term and come into work earlier, take courses and improve your skills, regularly read in your chosen field, focus in your work on high-value tasks because it will have a positive impact on your future.

Ask yourself these questions:
'What are my highest priority activities now?'
'What can I do if done well that will make a real difference?'
'What is the best use of my time right now?'
'What one skill if I developed it well would have the best impact on my life?'

Never stop improving because this decision can change your life.

Like the ancient proverb says: *"The journey of a thousand miles begins with a single step."* Remember this saying: to overcome procrastination and to achieve extraordinary things is to begin at once and to take the first step today to start your journey.

Choose any task, project or goal in your life that you have been procrastinating and write a list of all the steps you'll need to do to overcome the task. Then, take the first step and so on.

Do not allow a lack of ability or weakness to put you off because everything is learnable and if other people can do it, then so can you because you can learn this as well.

Upgrade Your Skills and Never Stop Learning

Steps to Mastery:

1. Get up earlier in the morning and read a magazine or book that will help you be more productive and effective in your career for at least 30 to 60 minutes each day.

2. Take every seminar, course or online training that can help you and attend business meetings, networking events and conferences of your profession or occupation. Aim to be one of the most knowledgeable people in your field, by continuing to learn and listen to audio recordings that will help you in all areas of your life.

3. Learn while you travel to work by listening to audio programmes in your car or on the bus, train, Tube or walking. The average car owner spends between 300 to 500 hours every year driving to work. You can become one of the highest paid, smartest and most capable people in your field just by listening to these audio programmes that will educate you as you drive around.

The more you learn, you'll feel more confident and motivated and the better you will become. There are no limits to what you can learn apart from the ones in your own imagination.

You have special talents and unique abilities which make you different from anyone else who has ever lived and that makes you remarkable. Think about your special talents and abilities and commit to becoming really good in those areas.

Ask yourself: "What do I do well that other people find difficult to do?" What are you good at? What has given you the most success in your work and life looking back on your career?

Ask: "What are the things in me that are holding me back?"

Imagine that you get an emergency message each day and you have to go away for a month starting tomorrow. So, what would you do today if you knew that you had to get it done before you leave? Whatever your answer is go ahead and do this right now.

Going to bed early each night, before midnight during the week days. Resting on weekends and taking one full day off without watching television, going on the Internet or using your computer or mobile phone will give you more energy, peace of mind and time to think creatively. This extra energy will help you to overcome procrastination so that you can get started on your most important tasks faster than if you were tired.

Aim to exercise for about 30 minutes each day and this can be walking to or from work or getting up earlier or taking a longer walk back home. Build this into your day as if it were a business appointment.

The better you feel about yourself when you start work, the less time you will procrastinate and the more focus you'll have to get the job done. Higher energy levels will lead to more happiness, more productivity and greater success in everything that you do.

If you have always dreamed about writing a book, then

commit to write one page a day or one chapter a day. I committed to writing this book within 30 days and so I set about every day to write one chapter or to add to each chapter as the inspiration came to me and I felt just like a tree this book began to grow with branches and it took me into different directions with new ideas and how I wanted to lay my thoughts out on every page. It was really exciting to do and to be able to create something out of nothing from my imagination and you can do this too.

You need to ask yourself one question "Am I in the nation of Procrastinator?" Because if you actually get out of your own way then you wouldn't have an excuse. Some people choose to fail because it's convenient and it keeps them from realising their objective and many people sabotage themselves because it's the path of least resistance.

Do It Now

It doesn't matter what you start to work on, just think of Nike and 'Just Do It'.

If you are feeling lazy, tell yourself that you are going to work on the task for 5 minutes and start on it right away. Then, keep working as if it's the most important thing to start and continue once you get going. Because standing still and doing nothing and putting it off for another time or day won't help you in making changes in your life.

One of the best ways to get yourself started is to repeat

these words over and over again: "Do it now."

If you feel yourself becoming distracted or slowing down or doing low-value activities, then repeat these words over and over again: "Back to work."

Whether you feel like it or not, self-discipline is the ability to force yourself to do what you should do. Once you begin, don't stop until you have 100 percent finished it.

"Never waste time because it is a precious thing."
— Laurence Lameche

Awaken Your Inner Hero Within 24 Hours

1. Start and finish important jobs and prioritise them by deciding what to do straight away and what to leave.
2. Ask yourself, "Are there potential consequences for starting or not doing this task?" Think about your decisions, choices and behaviour in your work and personal life.
3. To overcome procrastination, practise a 'do it now' attitude and tell yourself that you will do something for only 5 minutes, the secret is to start and then continue.

Focus

"You can manifest whatever you believe in!"
— Laurence Lameche

SECRET #10 to Awaken Your Inner Hero Within 24 Hours

The answer to all your problems lies within you. So, waste no time looking for peace, happiness, joy or contentment in the outside world. Have fun, love life and control your emotions and never allow anything to disturb your peace of mind and the pure love within you. And you will find something so rare that most people take a lifetime to find this hidden secret that lies within you.

Follow

One

Course

Until

Success

The world is filled with so many distractions from social media, television, phone calls, text messages, news and world events that are designed to distract you to lose focus.

So, I have learnt to pay attention to do one task at a time and only focus on that one thing until I complete it and then move onto the next one.

Control your mind on thoughts that are in your best interest with being careful what you pay attention to.

Remember that nothing in the past or in the future can harm you. Because one is gone and the other is unknown. Only the present can harm you.

Tip: When I feel that I am losing focus or have lost focus, I simply in that moment tap one finger to the side of my head and repeat the words 'Focus, Focus, Focus' and I get back to working on what I am meant to be focusing on in that moment.

If we focus on the good traits of people, instead of finding faults by thinking what we like about their character, we'll end up liking them more.

Set yourself 30, 60 or 90 minutes to work on your most important tasks until they are complete.

When you work, turn off notification alerts or noises that distract you and turn off your phone to eliminate all distractions so that you can work non-stop without any interruptions.

One of the best ways to do this is to wake up a few hours earlier when the world is quiet so that you can get so much more done in this time.

And reward yourself if there is something that was particularly painful to do by treating yourself to something nice (like reading this book again!)

If you want to change the outcome of many things in your life, start to focus on what you want rather than what you don't want and this success habit can completely change your life when your focus on the outcome rather than the obstacle.

Manifestations

A key secret to true mastery when it comes to manifestation, is how long you can hold the uninterrupted thought towards your desired intentions.

Be still in mind.

Be careful what you wish for, because it may come true.

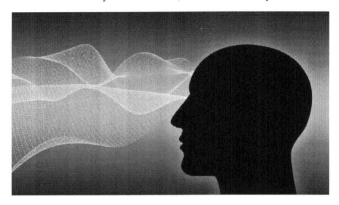

Practise Being More Productive Every Day

Declare to the universe that you'll do all you can to increase your income, strengthen your relationships, improve your health and to live life on your terms.

Ask yourself these questions:

1. Is this relationship or person moving me forward or backward?

2. Am I just busy or is what I am doing making me productive?

3. Is this activity preventing me from getting to the next level or making me money?

Are you like a fast car speeding down the road faster than everyone else, but you've not getting closer to your dreams or goals. Do you feel like a hamster trapped in a cage and on a wheel, running fast but getting nowhere?

You may be doing a lot of stuff that gives you the illusion that you are busy. But the things that you are doing are not making money or building a foundation to make this happen. You have got to ask yourself this question. "Is this activity making money for me or not?" You must decrease busyness/work that is not putting money in your pocket and instead replace it with increasing your money-making activities.

I know how hard it can be to change our habits and the way we think. But rather than going to see a psychologist every time I get a little voice in my head that says, "Do it later" I fight back this inner villain by ignoring my thoughts and then asking myself, "What would my inner hero do?" And the answer would be to take action immediately, even if at times it may be uncomfortable or painful to do. Every time I practise this, I find myself achieving a whole new level of life.

So how about implementing these habits as soon as you finish reading this chapter. Start on the areas of your life that you know need the most help with and ignore the thoughts begging you to put it off until "tomorrow" or "later" and instead take action today. Your habits will take you to where you want to go quicker than you can possibly imagine. Now is the best time to get started.

Don't put off until tomorrow, next week, next month or next year. Because there is no time like the present to start working on you today. So even if you are busy, stressed or you have a complex life, that is even more reason why you need to make these changes fast to improve your life.

Plan Your Day In Advance

Create a schedule and discipline yourself to do it. Because the most successful people and the greatest minds in history plan their day tomorrow, today.

I've met so many people over the years that talk the talk but don't walk the walk and what I mean by that is they talk about things they want to do, but never end up doing them.

Surround yourself with the right people. Schedule your day in advance and get things done. Focus your thoughts and if bad thoughts come up say "No" and switch to thinking the opposite positive thoughts to focus on success. Take action to get the results you want.

Ask yourself these questions:

1. Should I be doing this activity now?

2. Is it a waste of time?

3. Are these things moving me backward or forward?

If you want to start investing in property, but you are not sure whether to do this or not, ask yourself these questions: "Is it easy for me to do?", "Could this work for me?", "Do I think that I can do it?", "Do I need to know everything now before I start or can I learn along the way?", "Is this the right time?", "What if I have no money to invest in property?", "What if I can't get a mortgage?", "What if I don't have a job?", "What if I have bad credit?"

Well, these were the questions I thought many years ago, but I came out with a solution to acquire property without the need of a mortgage, deposit or needing a job. I had bad credit but I started to read books about how to do this and I attended real estate courses to develop these skills to then start acquiring property the easy way without needing a mortgage, deposit, job and having bad credit. Only you can decide whether you want to invest in the property business and make it a reality.

If you would like to learn how I did this, then you can buy a copy of my Amazon No.1 best-selling book today called '*How I Bought 3 London Properties For A Football Ticket.*' Go to this link now:
www.PropertyBookSecrets.com

Spend your time and energy doing high-priority tasks that are essential for your success.
- Look at the next 30 days to build the right momentum.
- List the order you need to get them done and then set deadlines.

It is really important to create a sense of urgency to set dates and deadlines. Successful people and entrepreneurs work best under pressure with a tight deadline within a reasonable window to get stuff done.

Time

Look at your time and become selfish with it. Imagine your income increasing and your problems decreasing.

If you get distracted during work hours, then you will lose the ability to create a legacy for the people you love.

To reduce distractions, decide who gets your attention when you work and commit yourself during these hours to the people and tasks who can help you take things to the next level. Stay focused in a world full of distraction.

Distractions could potentially cost you millions.

On average, people waste at least 30 minutes each day on social media which equals three and a half hours each week. This also happens when you add talking on the phone, emails, text messages, notifications, television, watching the news or reading articles. It all adds up to eventually costing you more money than you could possibly ever imagine.

Don't be accessible every hour of every day all the time. Ignore the alerts, bleeps, chimes or vibrations for notifications on Facebook and Instagram that you immediately feel the need to check it to see who liked and commented on your posts. People will soon notice that you don't text back straight away or answer their calls when they phone you or respond to emails instantly.

Promise yourself to not surf the Internet while you are working on your dreams, turn off the negativity in the news headlines and don't go to watch 50+ YouTube videos.

Only reply to emails maybe once or twice a day at a set time for a certain amount of time because otherwise it is a distraction throughout your day that you could do without. Maybe use an autoresponder that lets people know what time each day you will respond to emails.

Learn to say <u>NO</u> more than when you say Yes.

A Magic List For You

By taking one step at a time, you can get a promotion at work or get a new career, or sort out your finances and start a new business. You can start making these steps today. What emails need to be sent? What actions do you need to take? What negative friends do you need to get out of your life or what family members do you need to spend less time with? What people can you attract into your life? What certain things do you need to start saying "no" to? Start to write a list of the answers to these and other questions you can think of.

What tasks do you love to do? What skills or areas are you good at and what do you enjoy? What are the actions you need to take to achieve your financial goals? You can do this exercise for any part of your life. Take a look at your list.

Also, make another list of what not to do. This list is possibly more important to your success as you will see what things do not serve you for your future or help you to become the best version of yourself. Give up the old and welcome in the new habits to help you.

Here are some examples to help you identify what things to put on your not-to-do list.

1. Spending time with friends each week either on the phone or in person who are negative and bring nothing but doom and gloom into your life – you know who they are!

2. Paying a bill online and then wasting hours of your life spending time going online, watching videos and the negative news and looking at social media.

3. Procrastinating on a new business idea because you are not sure where to start.

4. Spending a lot of time on the sofa watching television, going to the gym (for too long), or talking to people who won't add value to your

life, just gossiping.

5. Doing chores in your home or, gardening, washing your car. These time-consuming activities could be given to someone else if you pay them to save you the time and energy to focus on achieving your biggest goals.

These non-important tasks should all be written on your not-to-do list and memorised so when they come up you know what not to do in future because these things are eating up your time and before you know it your life has flown by.

Write one or three things to the words below for your life:
Eliminate
Delegate
Replace
Automate
Outsource

For example, with the bill paying you could 'Automate' to pay all yours bills online through your bank. So, you might 'Automate' all your bills to be paid this way or 'Delegate' this to someone else in your family or maybe an employee or partner so they can take care of all the bills and check they have been paid once a month. For online surfing, replace this with researching how to achieve my goals, perhaps start to read about people in business that you admire or buying books that will teach you about marketing or sales, how to start a business with little money or great ways to improve and be more productive in your career or how to get a promotion. There are also many online courses that can help you learn valuable skills, techniques and processes that can start you on your journey to achieving your goals.

Replacing the wrong habits with new ones is easy when you have a plan that will empower you. You will then be able to figure out what areas of your life you want to get rid of on your not-to-do list and what's the best course of action to take to replace them with empowering habits that drive you forward on achieving more wealth, success, health and happiness.

If you focus your time on your own unique ability, the return on investment can be huge.

"The universe will help make your decisions happen, when you take action."
– Laurence Lameche

Awaken Your Inner Hero Within 24 Hours

1. In a world full of distractions, it is vital to focus on one task at a time.

2. If you feel like you are losing focus then repeat to yourself, 'Focus, focus, focus' and tap the side of your head gently with your finger when you say these words to remind yourself.

3. Is this activity preventing you from getting to the next level or making you money?

4. Ask yourself these questions; Should I be doing this activity now? Is it a waste of time? Are these things moving me backward or forward?

5. Plan your day in advance; ideally do this the day before.

6. Value your time and who you spend it with, avoid going on social media. watching television, surfing the internet or doing low value tasks.

Regrets

"Risks are opportunities in life you didn't take, that later become regrets."
— Laurence Lameche

SECRET #11 to Awaken Your Inner Hero Within 24 Hours

When life knocks you down, do your best not to think about it and move on as quickly as possible because everything in life is a test. And the secret is how well we deal with this. No one wins all the time and so turn your failures into lessons to grow. Never give up. Your time will come.

When I am faced with a difficult decision, I think to myself: 'Would I regret not making this decision at some point in the future?' Say, for example, your dream is to be an actor, singer, sports athlete, set up a business, be in a loving relationship, have a family, travel the world.

Whenever you are not sure whether to do something or not, ask yourself this question: "Would I regret more going for my goal or dream and failing, or not even going for it at all?"

My answer is almost always the same, that I would much rather 'go for it' than give up on my dreams and wonder what could've been.

So, ask yourself the same question. It's worked for me in convincing me to 'just do it' and 'go for it'.

You can't change your past, so don't stress about it. It was simply development and research for the great things ahead of you.

Opportunity

How you view the world depends on your mental attitude. You can choose to focus on doubt, fear and failure. Or you can focus on your strengths in finding courage, confidence and success.

When you do not allow others to determine your future and when you refuse to allow for setbacks to defeat you, you are destined for success.

So many people miss opportunity when it comes knocking on their door because they are too busy down at their local convenience store buying lottery tickets.

How many times do you remember having a great idea but not acting upon it, only to later find out that someone else used the same idea and turned it into a business.

Make a commitment to yourself to start to take action when you have a good idea.

Don't wait for things to happen, make them happen!

Opportunities appear to those who have dreams and goals and also a plan for making them happen.

Every time you face a difficult problem, stop and think for a moment and ask yourself: *"Is there an opportunity hidden within this problem?"* When you find the answer, you'll be ahead of your competitors.

> *"If you want a new life, start making decisions."*
> — Laurence Lameche

Failure and Defeat Time To Make A New Start

It may not seem easy when you come across a challenging situation. So, remember that you always have a choice how best to deal with it in life with the power of how to use the thoughts in your mind. The experience you gain from making mistakes should be put to good use to not make them again. No matter where you are now, remember that whatever you believe in your mind you can achieve it.

You are either moving forward or going backwards in life.

Don't Waste Time With People Who Messed Up Their Lives

Be careful with the people you spend time with because if they have messed up their lives and blame others for their misfortune, then they aren't the kind of people to help you achieve success in your life. So, choose your friends carefully and do your best not to complain about your life, an individual, your company or job. Spend time with positive people who are ambitious and optimistic about their lives.

Learn From Failure Otherwise You're None The Wiser

If you refuse to learn from history, then you are doomed to repeat it. If we don't learn from our failures, then we are likely to repeat them until we learn from our experiences. Or give up and we can accept defeat as permanent failure. Every setback in life has valuable information if you look for the clues that can eventually lead to your success.

Without adversity there is no wisdom, and without wisdom, success is short-lived. If you make a mistake, say to yourself, "That's good – at least I've gotten that out of the way and I won't be doing that again."

Life is a constant lesson, but when you learn to not let 'mistakes' bother you because you treat them as learning experiences, it will not seem like a roller coaster of highs and lows.

Going The Extra Mile: When The Going Gets Tough

If you think achieving success is easy, you don't understand how this process works or you've set your sights too low. Reaching the top in any profession is difficult, time-consuming and slow. Most people won't do what is necessary to achieve success because they are too willing to give up when it gets tough.

If you want to be inspired, then learn about the lives of men and women who have achieved great success by reading their biographies and listening to audio books of their lives.

They all succeeded because they never quit and they continued to move forward on their dreams long after others had given up.

Going the extra mile is learning to be better in all that you do.

Your power of imagination is to visualise solutions to difficult problems and to create new ideas, and see yourself accomplishing the goals you've set yourself.

It Takes Courage To Act

When I left school, my first ever job was as a door-to-door salesman for a double-glazing company booking appointments to sell windows.

It was really tough, getting the door slammed in your face, and being shouted at and told to go away, and to hear "No, No, No, No."

"Going from failure without ever losing enthusiasm
is real courage."
– Laurence Lameche

I learned to step into my fears and push myself. I went to the next door and said, "Would you like new windows and doors?" and was told "NO!" and they slammed the door again. So I went to the next door: "NO" again, and "NO" again and again and again. After a while, I no longer took it personally.

I started to play a game with myself telling myself, "I am sure someone will say 'Yes' to me and I am not going back home at night until I get a 'Yes'."

I continued to knock on doors and eventually someone said, "Yes," and then I said, "Are you sure?" You must find the courage to face your fears and continue to push through even when things are tough.

I used to run to each door to get there before my colleagues and I would sometimes end up knocking on double the amount of doors than anyone else who I used to work with and I thought this would increase my chances to speak to more people and therefore I would stand a much better chance of someone saying YES to me!

"Learn to pick yourself back up when you fall. If you can't, then please call 999, 911 or 112 depending on what country you're in."
– Laurence Lameche

Awaken Your Inner Hero Within 24 Hours

1. For regrets, imagine how you would feel at the end of your life and looking back on things, to help you make an important decision now. Ask yourself how you would feel if you chose to do or not do something important. Would you have any regrets? Weigh it up and make the decision.

2. Opportunities appear to those who have dreams and plan for them to happen.

3. Be careful who you spend time with because you become the average of the five people who you spend the most time with.

4. Learn by your failures to not make the same mistakes again.

5. *Remember: "Winners never quit, and quitters never win."*

Positive Mental Attitude

"Every day is a new day to start a new life."
— Laurence Lameche

SECRET #12 to Awaken Your Inner Hero Within 24 Hours

Yesterday is history, tomorrow's a mystery but today is a gift, which is why it's the present. While sometimes life is not fair, never allow the moment to change your attitude or plans that you have for your future. You cannot win if you feel sorry for yourself – just dust yourself down, pick yourself up and carry on because your future needs you!

You must think of yourself as the most important person alive. No one is going to die for you so why would you want to live for them.

Believe in yourself and work on developing your

character and continue to look at ways you can improve throughout your life day by day, week by week, month by month and year by year. Believe that you will succeed at what you choose to do.

We are spiritual beings having human experiences.

We are here to enjoy life. We can't always control the events in our lives but we can choose to control how we react to them.

Learn how to react to things good and bad. The goal is to be better and to always improve and evolve in life to be the greatest version of ourselves that we can be.

Ignorance is the root of all suffering in your life.

Temporary setbacks help you to learn from defeat and to prepare you for success when it arrives.

Treat everyone the way you want to be treated. Be kind to others, smile at strangers and be loving.

If you want more love, be more loving.

If you want more money, give it away to attract more.

If you don't want people to gossip about you, then don't gossip about others.

Think about the person who you wish to become. Someone who is happy, positive, kind, heathy, successful and to fulfil all your dreams and goals in life. Who are you?

Why are you here?

What is your purpose?

Have A Positive Mental Attitude

In every situation, look for the good. Whatever went wrong, look for the good in something and you'll find it.

What valuable lesson did I learn from this experience or setback? If you can see the valuable lesson in each obstacle or setback, you'll grow from it.

Instead of complaining or blaming, look for the solution in every problem when things go wrong. Ask questions like: "What can we do now?", "What next step can we take?" and "What is the solution?"

Talk about your dreams and goals and think about how to achieve them. Think about your future and don't dwell on the past because you can't drive a car by looking in the rear-view mirror. Look forward not backwards.

Make sure you feed your mind with positive thoughts, just like your body needs regular exercise and healthy foods.

It's equally important to not focus on worry or fear of failure as this could make you ill, because the mind will bring into your reality what you think about most.

Your Mental Attitude Towards Defeat

Ask yourself these questions: What can I do differently next time that would have given me a different outcome?

How can I minimise problems and mistakes in the future? What can I do next time to learn from this experience?

By asking yourself these questions, you'll be surprised how quickly you can turn defeat into victory by overcoming these obstacles and setbacks in the future.

Time to give up friends or people you know who are constantly negative. "But what if they are members of my family?" I hear you say?

Then look to find ways to spend less time with them or if it's the holiday season and you have to be around these people, then maybe buy EarPods and put them in your ears so you can listen to audio books, motivational talks, online training or affirmations and occasionally nod when you are with them. Problem solved – you're welcome!

"Run away from negative people because negativity is contagious."
– Laurence Lameche

Spend time with happy people, who are positive. Your time is a precious asset, so spend it wisely with people who want to succeed and encourage you with your dreams and goals in life.

How To Have An Abundant Attitude

Here is my list of what to do to have an abundant attitude so that you can create your own daily living routine in order to increase and attract good things into your life and so that your goals and dreams come true at a quicker rate.

A: Abundance in thoughts, feelings, and actions

B: Believe in yourself and in your dreams

C: Create a magical life

D: Determination to succeed

E: Excitement to live your dream life

F: Focus on your goals

G: Grow and learn

H: Hope there is always hope

I: Imagine what is possible

J: Just do it now

K: Kindness to kittens and to yourself

L: Laugh because life is meant to be fun

M: Motivation to make it happen.

N: Never give up.

O: Optimistic for the future

P: Positive mind

Q: Quitters never win

R: Risk challenge yourself every day

S: Success be the superhero you were born to be

T: Thank you for having the time to enjoy life

U: Unique and special are words to describe you

V: Visualize in your dreams and goals in life

W: Wealth and Wisdom

X: X-factor—you have it, so use your talent.

Y: Yes, you can do it

Z: Zest for life

"The greatest power on the planet that we all own is our mind." – Laurence Lameche

Awaken Your Inner Hero Within 24 Hours

1. Treat everyone the way you want to be treated.
2. Look for the good in every situation.
3. What could have I done differently next time that would have given me a different outcome?
4. Remember to control your thoughts. Because what you think about most of the time you become, so make sure you are thinking and talking about what you want rather than what you don't want.
5. Keep positive by accepting complete responsibility for everything that happens to you. Don't blame, complain or criticise others for anything. Make progress rather than excuses. Focus your energy and thoughts on moving forward on ways you can improve your life right now and let go of the rest.
6. Have an abundant attitude to life and create your own daily living routine in order to increase and attract good things into your life.

Knowledge

"Knowledge always pays the best return on investment." – Laurence Lameche

SECRET #13 to Awaken Your Inner Hero Within 24 Hours

Treat everyone as if they are going to die at midnight. Whether they are a loved one or stranger, friend or enemy, show that person the kindness, care and understanding of how you would like to be treated. Your life will never be the same again, so in a world where you can choose to be anything choose to be kind.

Knowledge Is not power unless you use it.

Learn Something New Each Day

If you're not learning in your job, you are falling behind. It's impossible to stand still because you are either moving forward or going backwards in your chosen career. Look at each day as a good opportunity to learn something new, grow, and to improve yourself and to do things better than you've ever done them before.

The Cost Of Getting Bad Advice

Getting bad advice could cost you more than you could imagine. Just think about it for a second: have you ever had a good idea that could change the world, a thought or invention that could make money? But then when you told a friend or family member or even a loved one, they give you a reason why they think it will never work.

Sometimes we listen to the wrong advice – let me give

you an example. Would you want to get advice from a jobless person spending their day in the pub on setting up a new business? Or would you ask a single friend about relationships? And would you ask your broke friends to tell you how you should make money? This is why bad advice could cost you a lot, so be careful who you listen to.

Bad advice feeds your inner villain and you end up playing it safe because it stops you from taking the actions to pursue the life you really desire. By listening to this dream-stealing advice, you are not encouraging your inner hero to live life on your terms.

It is important to understand that sometimes the people we love want to protect us from getting hurt and failing. Maybe your spouse is afraid that if you change, it may affect your relationship? Maybe co-workers don't want you to get ahead of them, or your boss might be afraid you'll end up taking their job. Maybe a friend had a painful relationship that ended badly and wants to protect you. Or a relative lost a business and doesn't want you to make the same mistake they did. Some people may want to sabotage on purpose, but most people feel they are protecting you from being hurt yet in fact they are simply feeding your inner villain by creating doubt in your mind and knocking your confidence.

So, by being aware of this bad advice 24/7, you can protect yourself and prevent it getting into your mind when someone is speaking to you. Because bad advice has cost me a lot in my life as I am sure it has for you, but don't worry because you are not alone.

Be careful about getting advice from people who have

failed in what you want to do. It might be tempting to think you want to learn from their mistake, but they can only teach you how to do it wrong, so it's not worth it.

So, if you ignore people who give bad advice and only get good advice from people who are qualified. By not feeding your inner villain, your confidence will grow.

"Knowledge is power if you take action on what you learn." – Laurence Lameche

 Awaken Your Inner Hero Within 24 Hours

1. Learn something new each day that will benefit your life.
2. Getting bad advice could end up costing you a lot, so be careful whose advice you listen to.

See The Good In Every Situation

"Always see the seed of good in every unpleasant situation." — Laurence Lameche

SECRET #14 to Awaken Your Inner Hero Within 24 Hours

Look for the good in every unpleasant situation. It will help you in your darkest days to see the light at the end of the tunnel. Things are bought into our lives to test us and to teach us to follow the right path in discovering who we really are meant to be. Sometimes clues are hidden in plain sight for our greater good. Everything happens for a reason.

According to society I wasn't meant to become a success because I didn't do well at school and I had no money. But I didn't let that put me off even though my teachers never thought that I would amount to anything. 'Well, I'll show them,' I thought. And so, I did.

I was lucky when I was a child because I failed a lot and so failure doesn't really bother me anymore!

I didn't know anyone who was rich and I didn't have a mentor who could teach me the secrets to life and how to be successful. I disliked reading when I was younger. I was told to work on my weaknesses – which I now realise could have left me full of self-doubt and frustration – rather than to concentrate on my strengths, which seems obvious now. But that's what we should be taught to focus on: what we are actually good at. It makes sense doesn't it?

A few years ago, I wrote my first book called *'How I Bought 3 London Properties For A Football Ticket'* which become an international bestseller. The only reason I decided to write the book was because when people used to ask me, *"What do you do for work?"* I would reply, *"Imagine owning a home you'd love to own, but didn't think you can afford. Well I help people just like you with families like yours who want to buy a property without the need of a mortgage, you don't need a deposit, you don't even need to have a job and you can actually have bad credit but still get on the property ladder. Would you like to learn how?"*

And because so many people were really interested to learn more and to find out how this works I decided to write a book because I wanted to help as many people around the world discover the secret that the banks don't want you to know about – that the rich want to keep hidden from ordinary people just like you and me. I don't think that is fair, so I decided to write a book that actually works in the real world for the good of the people.

I've learnt that I have an ability to write and deliver a message that is simple yet effective, that anyone can understand no matter what your background may be or where you are from. Because I don't teach theory, I teach practical, easy-to-learn step-by-step processes that help people to take action so they can transform their circumstances.

Although when I started to write my book, I have to admit that I did have a little self-doubt creep into my thoughts of 'you failed school; you find reading challenging; you don't use big words' because you don't understand most of them.' And my teachers used to criticise me because of my speling. I guess now I had the last laugh, Mrs Green!

But I knew this villain inside me was testing me, so I

had to learn to get out of my own way and block out those thoughts by telling myself that I have a message to deliver to the world which will be my legacy. Also, if anything happened to me I wanted my son, who was a baby at the time, to read my book one day to get to know who his father was and to learn more about my life and to give him something to be proud of and also to learn these secrets one day to help him in his life, just like I wanted to help you.

So, these were some of the reasons that drove me to continue to write my first book until I finished it and not to give up when things started to get tough along the way. I am so proud of that book because it has helped to change many lives around the world. If you want to get your FREE copy, all you need to do is to pay for shipping and handling, go to this website now: **www.PropertyBookSecrets.com**

I started writing my book many years ago, but life seemed to get in the way at the time so I put it off and kept telling myself, "Oh, I will write it next year." Until one day I told myself "enough is enough" and I wrote my first book within 5 days. You might be wondering, 'How did you do this?' Well, I am glad you asked me this question, because I spoke to other successful authors who I thought were too busy to write a book and when I found out their secret, I just took action and applied their knowledge and wisdom to get my book written quickly in the same way. You see the answer is always out there, you just have to look for it sometimes, without having to reinvent the wheel.

This book however took me 30 days to write, but I applied a different approach to writing this book from how I wrote my first book. It doesn't matter if I'm not a trained writer because I believe that I do have a powerful message that can help change the lives of many people around the world and I am glad to be sharing this knowledge with you.

By questioning yourself based on your flaws that you think you have, or perhaps others have told you about, you are feeding this inner villain, and this stops you from taking up other opportunities that may pass you by over the years. If you could instead work on your strengths, it will help you to overcome any weaknesses. Everyone is good at something, so concentrate on that.

You have amazing gifts and unique abilities inside you and your success depends on improving your greatness by making it a habit.

Remember the story of the two wolves? Well, the one you feed wins. So, if you put energy into something that you're not good at, then you will lose confidence and move further away from success. However, if you focus on things that you are good at, you'll become great at them. Then you can pay someone else to do the things you're not good at. This will help to improve every area of your life, along with your bank balance. If you really want to build financial success and wealth, then make it a habit of only focusing on all the things that you do well.

"The destiny of the earth is up to us and its fate is in our hands." — Laurence Lameche

---

 Awaken Your Inner Hero Within 24 Hours

1. See the good in every situation.
2. Focus on your strengths.
3. There is a book inside you: start writing about your life's experiences because your knowledge is valuable and you could help others with your story.

Thoughts – Be Careful
What You Think

"The ripple effect starts when you change your thoughts, words and actions – you'll experience a new world of possibilities that will open up to you."
– Laurence Lameche

SECRET #15 to Awaken Your Inner Hero Within 24 Hours

Thoughts become things, so be really careful with the thoughts that enter your mind. This may be one of the most powerful lessons in life to learn and to implement it every day. If you believe it, you can achieve it. So, if you can imagine it in your mind, you can manifest it to become a reality in your life. Create something magical today – use the power of thought to change your life forever. The great secret in life is that thoughts become things. Think about your dream life, plant your seeds and trust they will grow, have faith that they will blossom.

When you wake up in the morning, think this: *'I'm getting up to do the things that are the reason why I exist and that I was bought into this world to do. Or is my purpose to lay in bed under the covers and keep warm?'*

Because thoughts become things. So, pay careful attention to your thoughts because they are very powerful and you are manifesting what you think whether that's Positive or Negative and then it becomes your reality. So, if you catch yourself thinking something that you don't want, say "Stop!" and replace that thought with a better thought or affirmation.

Or put an elastic band on your wrist and every time you catch yourself thinking a negative thought, pull the band so it gently flicks your wrist so you feel pain. After a while, it will train your mind that a negative thought equals pain, so you will hopefully stop doing this to yourself.

Thoughts become things. So, for every thought you think, whether it's good or bad, it's a form of energy. So, your thoughts affect you. If you think about success, you condition your mind to attract more success into your life. The same is true if you think about failure, you'll attract that into your life.

So, keep your mind on track to only focus on good thoughts and when you notice negative thoughts appearing, stop them and replace those thoughts with positive ones.

Stop thinking about your problems and start focusing on the solutions and what you are grateful for in your life. This will enable you to start to manifest what you really want into your reality.

Be careful because the universe is listening. Your words are so powerful.

The root of all your problems in your life is coming from within you and the only thing keeping you from your inner greatness is overcoming your inner villain. You can have every single thing you focus on. Learn to become the greatest version of yourself by focusing on the "you" in the mirror and making that change.

Be mindful of what you are thinking, because your thoughts are very important and they do manifest. Think about what you love, desire and are in gratitude for and what you want to manifest in your life. Be mindful of your thoughts and what you don't like. Remember to focus on good thoughts.

Control Your Thoughts

To boost your self-esteem, talk to yourself positively all the time by saying affirmations like "I like myself" over and over again until you start to believe it and you will act like a person who has a high-performance personality.

To overcome feelings of fear or doubt, say to yourself, "I can do it". When people ask, "How are you doing?" Always reply with, "I feel wonderful." These things will help keep you motivated.

Creative Ideas

Think creatively for about 5 to 25 minutes per day. This is how I came up with the idea for this book because I ask myself this question every day: *"What creative idea can I think of today, that can help the lives of many people around the world?"* I then came up  with the inspiration for the name of the book title and then the ideas started to appear in my mind.

Ask Yourself These Questions

- What creative ideas can I think of today that will help people around the world?

- What can I do today, that can change my world tomorrow?

Ask yourself in the morning, *"What great ideas can I think of today that can improve me and that will empower me to reach my goal?"*

One idea can change your life!

"Your thoughts are like seeds in the garden of your mind. So, do you choose to grow flowers or weeds?"
— Laurence Lameche

Awaken Your Inner Hero Within 24 Hours

1. Thoughts become things. So be careful what you think about all the time.

2. Only focus on the good, positive thoughts and not the bad thoughts because the universe is listening to everything you think about which is manifesting whether you like it or not.

3. To overcome feelings of fear and doubt say, "I can do it."

4. If people ask you how are you doing reply: "I feel wonderful"

5. Think creatively every day and ask yourself, "What idea can I think of today, that can help empower the lives of many people around the world?' By asking myself this question over several weeks I came up with the idea and inspiration for this book, title, chapters and content.

Use Your Mind Wisely

"When you fill your mind with positive thoughts, it has great power and your life will never be the same again."
— Laurence Lameche

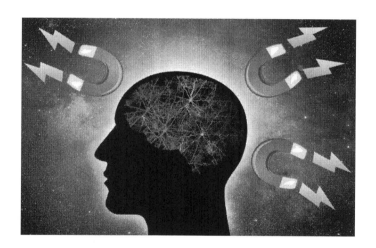

SECRET #16 to Awaken Your Inner Hero Within 24 Hours

Count your blessings every day. Because once you realise how special you really are and how many things you have got going for you, you'll start to shine, your confidence will return and you will be unstoppable.

Your mind is the most powerful asset you have. Spend at least 30 minutes a day on studying, reading, thinking and planning. Continue to review your short-term and long-term goals and ask yourself whether you are you on schedule. What information do you need to help you to complete your goal? Then, take action immediately to get this information. Because your future is waiting to celebrate you.

Play the "What if?" game to win by focusing on solutions and not problems. No matter how serious your problems are and if they keep you awake at night, remind yourself that for every problem there is a solution.

Through the power of thought, you can improve any situation in which you find yourself. But you can also destroy a positive life by thinking negatively.

A negative mind will always look for ways it can't be done, but a positive mind will always find a way it can be done.

If you repeat your words often and with belief, your subconscious mind is going to believe anything you tell it.

If you can imagine it in your mind, you can also create it into your reality.

Your mind is being controlled to suppress you from living your optimal life by your inner villain, that's why you need to break free. So, you can gain control again of your life and awaken your inner hero from within.

Time to stop these inner forces wanting to stop you and set yourself free.

Your Greatest Assets Are The Thoughts You Think About

What you think about most, you become. If you allow your mind to think about trivial matters, your achievements will likely be unimportant. So, concentrate on thinking important thoughts that will empower you in your life. Keep up to date with new things in your field. Think about finding a solution to any problem by making a list of good ideas to use anytime. Remember that small minds talk about people, average minds talk about events and great minds think about ideas.

"Which inner voice do you listen to (who said that)?
Listen to the 'good' and ignore the 'bad' just like
the 'Two Wolves' story earlier."
— Laurence Lameche

 Awaken Your Inner Hero Within 24 Hours

1. Spend 30 minutes a day studying, reading, thinking and planning to use your most valuable asset — your mind.
2. Review short-term and long-term goals.
3. You have the power to improve any situation with the power of your thoughts.

Working For Yourself

"If you can dream it, do it — Believe in yourself, have Courage and Determination to begin at once."
— Laurence Lameche

SECRET #17 to Awaken Your Inner Hero Within 24 Hours

The secret to living a wonderful, stress-free life is not to react to stressful situations and to think of them simply as a test that our inner villain wants us to go through from time to time during our lives. Because stress kills and it is slowly killing you, your mind, body and spirit. But imagine that your inner hero wants you to live in a peaceful state within, no matter whatever the situation that happens around you or internally that makes you feel stressed. Don't take life too seriously and learn to have fun. Learn how to respond to these situations as an opportunity to grow.

Looking back on all the different businesses I've set up, my advice would be to think about the problems that you have overcome in your life and ask yourself: can you help other people with the same solution?

So, keep thinking to yourself: "How can I help other people overcome the same problems I have overcome in my life and can I monetise this?' By building websites, funnels, posting and advertising on social media, learning about advertising, marketing and sales – or getting other people or companies to help you do this – you can position yourself as an expert and start to promote your idea to the world.

Rules To Business Manners

1. Dress to Impress.
2. Look people in the eye when you shake their

hand (with a firm handshake) and smile.

3. Always pause for a second when a person finishes talking, then you can speak.
4. Compliment people.
5. Listen to someone speaking without looking at your phone.
6. Be positive, cheerful and happy.
7. Speak kindly about others.
8. Remember names.
9. Always be kind.
10. Do not speak about religion, politics or money.
11. If you can listen to what the person does and think about how you can help them in their company by introducing them to another mutually beneficial person or company, this is an excellent way to build trust.

Opportunity and choice can sometimes overwhelm us in this busy world and we can end up doing nothing. If you sit all day waiting for things to change but do nothing about it, then nothing is going to happen.

"Be kind to each other and treat people the way you would like to be treated. Smile, listen and be friendly. Remember that we are all connected."
– Laurence Lameche

Successful Entrepreneurs

Our strong leaders who make decisions and take control of situations build a great team and surround themselves with the best people. Don't be afraid to appear unreasonable to get what you want. Be bold not cautious, and use your intuition.

Some entrepreneurs put their lives on hold for many years and struggle financially not being able to pay themselves any salary in the early days. Whilst working hard seven days a week, sometimes their health and relationships are at risk in their pursuit of a better life and chasing their dreams. And many only started living when they became rich. But you get nowhere without taking risks.

You'll get amazing results if you mix enthusiasm with passion and intensity.

If you have a willingness to learn from others, find out what works and then improve it. Unleash the power within you to take a new idea and then you can change the world forever.

Better Way Of Doing Anything

The most valuable ideas in any type of business are those that make money, save time, save money, or improve how things are done. Every improvement is a step in the right direction. To think of creative ideas, you must be positive as you think of ways to improve your performance, to find a better, quicker or more effective way to perform a task or build a product. Work out the risks and focus on the possibilities.

In the darkest hours, take comfort that this is a test in

life to strengthen your character to prepare you for your future, so be prepared to take on greater challenges.

The one person who knows what is best for you in the world is you.

The best way to get practical experience is to get working on your idea.

Faith and Hope

Remember that you can always seek help and advice because no problem is unique or new.

To find tomorrow's innovations, think about the trends that may affect your business or how your customers will think.

We can always find the answer to the problem with experience if we analyse the situation to develop a response.

Imagine talking to God from within or the universe or your creator or whatever you believe in. Well your soul is pure and it is divine wisdom.

Start With Enthusiasm, Commitment & Determination

So, stop dreaming about your idea and take action to make it happen now. Then inspire others with your dream and be bold enough to begin right away.

Do not give up when others are involved in your inspiring future. Stay committed and change your approach if you need to. Because if you fail, it's better to fail if others have stopped you and not because you stopped yourself.

To get big ideas out in the world it takes ordinary people to do extraordinary things.

Sacrifices

For the next few years, you may need to make sacrifices in your life in order to have a better life in the future. This future may be potentially within the next five years. So, you need to start to say "no" to many things that are not going to help you with your goal. So, watch less television and the news, limit yourself to how long you spend on social media each day, limit the time you spend with friends and family on the phone and in person.

Perhaps you have to cancel your holiday plans for the next few years. If you are in a relationship, explain what you are doing for your partner to understand and if they don't then perhaps, they are not the person you are looking to be with and you will need to move on. After you finish work during the day at 5pm or 6pm, then come home and work from 8pm until 1am, you only live once. Nothing happens overnight. Think about sacrificing short-term pleasure for long-term gain.

My hope is that you take action and apply the knowledge and ideas inside these pages to your own life.

Reward

Reward yourself for the long hours or for achieving your goal or doing something that is challenging. For example, if you are a sales person, setting yourself a daily target for phone calls and once you've achieved it, give yourself a treat.

"To see the light you must first go through darkness. If it continues, then go see an optician."
— Laurence Lameche

 Awaken Your Inner Hero Within 24 Hours

1. Think of the problems that you have overcome in your life and can you monetise this by helping other people overcome the same problems?
2. Dress to impress because you never get a second chance to make the first impression.
3. Surround yourself with the best people who can help you build your dreams.
4. Most valuable ideas in any type of business are those that make money, save time, save money, or improve how things are done.
5. There is always an answer to every problem.
6. Make sacrifices to work on your dreams.
7. Reward yourself when you work hard.

Change Of Direction

"Don't stand and wait for greatness to happen — go out and find it even if you have to change direction."
— Laurence Lameche

SECRET #18 to Awaken Your Inner Hero Within 24 Hours

It's just a change of direction: be flexible and go along for the ride. Remember that life is a journey full of bumps along the road and sometimes it takes us in unexpected directions that we have to adapt to rather than fighting against the changes. Sometimes it is better to adapt our approach to what life has in store for us – it's not a problem, let the changes flow and embrace the unexpected journey that is life.

Imagine that life happens for us and not to us. Life sometimes tests us in many ways and we have to go with the flow just as if we were in a paddle boat on the river and the current took us in a direction we didn't expect – would we paddle upstream against the current or carry on in the new direction and see where it goes?

When entrepreneurs start a new business, the original idea doesn't always work out as planned. I remember when I started my first business in London in the nightclub industry to help people get VIP entry into three different nightclubs for the price of one in one night with a free drink for £10, skip the queue and saving them money on the door price.

I approached different hotels and concierges in London to hand out flyers and tell them about the idea to get them to sell tickets. After working hard for 7 days, I only had 6 people who turned up on the first night. When I took them to the first club, I waited with my sign in the middle of Piccadilly Circus and after about 10 minutes, people started to come up to me asking me what was on offer: I sold another 10 tickets within 30 minutes. Then, I thought rather than just waiting for people to come up to me, I should walk up to them and ask them if they wanted to go to a night club tonight and get VIP entry.

This started to work out well. So I thought if I could spend more time doing this and develop a street team of 10 to 20 people who I could train to approach people, this would be more worthwhile than spending my time going to every hotel in London and doing it all by myself. And this is what I did – which wasn't what I was expecting at all – but I knew I had to evolve in concentrating on what worked.

Then, I decided to leave the nightclub industry and go into property without any experience. I bought my first investment property in central London the traditional way with a mortgage and a deposit. Then, I rented it out as a holiday let – because I was a former tour guide on the open-top buses, I thought that this could be a great holiday let near to King's Cross station which it was for many years.

But then I ran out of money, so I started to think creatively. I kept asking myself, "How can I acquire more property in London without the need of a mortgage or a deposit and help landlords get rid of their property problems?" And I started to acquire properties for £1 without the need of a mortgage or a deposit and you don't need a job or good credit to do this. People couldn't believe what I was doing, which was controlling properties this way, so I wrote my first

book which became an international best-seller *called 'How I Bought 3 London Properties For A Football Ticket'* — go to the link to find out more:
www.PropertyBookSecrets.com

Then, I started to use a strategy called Rent2Rent, which means I rented properties from landlords and letting agents, and then I used to sub-let them to make a profit by renting them as serviced accommodation to tourists and business travellers.

As a hobby, for many years I have been going to sold-out concerts and sporting events without a ticket. I have figured out a way to buy cheaper tickets to sold-out concerts and sporting events. I've now developed a 3-step proven process to help other people around the world get the same results — guaranteed.

To get immediate access now to my live training videos where I hold your hand every step of the way through this easy and transferable process:
www.TicketsOnDemand.live

Then, I developed another online training to help landlords let their vacant properties using only social media and without a letting agent:
www.PropertyRentalSecrets.co.uk

Because I am a shy person and an introvert by nature, I find it challenging to approach people at networking events, business conferences and training events. So, if you find it challenging like me to network with people at these events, I have come up with a quick way to network with lots of people and to collect as many business cards as possible without talking to them and it works every time, for everyone at every event.

If you would like to learn 'How To Network Without Talking To People' then I have developed a 3-step process to **Present** yourself in a way that's unforgettable. To **Persuade** people who wouldn't normally give you the time of day and to **Profit** from the new connections you make for a lifetime. Get access to all my training videos here:
www.NetworkingSecretsOnline.com

When you ride the current in a certain direction that you didn't expect it to go, then maybe it will lead you to success. When you let go of specific outcomes, the weight of expectation is lifted off your shoulders. Your happiness will skyrocket and you become a better person. For years, I have wanted to work on turning these ideas into an online training, book, funnel, website or live event to help people just like you with families like yours and that has been what I have been working on for most of my life. I like to continually challenge myself with each new decade that passes, so I feel I am growing and evolving with the times as I get older.

Change

Nothing gets better until you change. No one is going to change for you, so you have to see the advantage of changing for yourself. If you do not change, you will stay where you are.

Don't wait like most people for the start of a new year to make a New Year's resolution because we all have the ability to make a decision anytime that will improve the quality of our lives.

Be willing to change and do it quickly to survive long-term.

"It's easy to think about changing the world, but few think about changing themselves."
— Laurence Lameche

 Awaken Your Inner Hero Within 24 Hours

1. Sometimes life takes you on a change of direction. When that happens it is important to adapt and embrace change, rather than to fight against it.

Forgiveness

"Not forgiving someone is like drinking poison yourself and hoping the other person is going to die."
— Laurence Lameche

SECRET #19 to Awaken Your Inner Hero Within 24 Hours

If you want to live longer, heal disease and live a happy life then you need to learn to forgive people, yourself and situations. It doesn't matter if your reason is justified because they did something wrong or you are upset with them. The reason we forgive people is for our own inner well-being and not for them. Forgive and learn to let go to be at peace with yourself. I know it is easier said than done, but it truly is in our best interest to forgive.

Not forgiving someone is like drinking poison and expecting the other person to die.

Holding a grudge is allowing a person to live rent-free in your head. Holding onto unforgiveness, is like thinking that you are doing the other person harm. When in fact unforgiveness does much more harm to you, than to the other person.

Forgiveness is a choice not an option and it is not easy. C. S. Lewis said that everyone thinks that forgiveness is a lovely idea until they have something to forgive and then it is really hard.

It's true that the first to apologise is the bravest, the first to forgive is the strongest and the first to forget is the happiest.

If God forgives, you must forgive yourself.

Can you forgive your enemies? When I think 'no I don't think I can' I imagine Jesus on the cross saying

"Father, forgive them, for they know not what they do." And I think if Jesus could forgive while nailed to the cross, then why should I want to hold that resentment inside me? I should just let it go and forgive because, after all, it is for your own good that you do.

Now, you don't have to be religious to understand this concept but this has helped me in my life and so I thought it was important to share this with you.

I am still learning to love my enemies; it is not easy. But it is important to me to learn to develop inner peace by forgiving.

"A true hero isn't judged by their power, strength or courage but instead by their heart."
— Laurence Lameche

Awaken Your Inner Hero Within 24 Hours

1. It may be challenging but learn to forgive to live longer, heal disease and for your own well-being and inner peace.

Goals

"Dreams come true, if you have them!"
— Laurence Lameche

SECRET #20 to Awaken Your Inner Hero Within 24 Hours

Set goals each day that will take you a step closer towards your dream. Write them down and get to work at once on your number one task today. It will help you to plan what you are doing the day before you start your day, so that you know exactly what you need to work on tomorrow in advance. This will save you time as failure to do this can result in the day, week, month and year just drifting away without you working on what really matters.

Set daily, weekly, monthly and yearly goals. Make sure to achieve those by working on them all the time. But remember that Rome wasn't built in a day – so whatever you are working on, know that it may take time to get there.

Write your goals down on paper with a pen.

I build this into my day after waking up and brushing my teeth. I then think and talk out loud about all the goals I want to achieve this month, the next few months, this year, next year and in the future. I do this for 15 to 30 minutes first thing in the morning before I do anything else.

Then, after about one or two hours, I will go for a walk around my neighbourhood for 30 minutes: I think about all the goals I want to achieve in my life – some of the goals I think about are financial, family, health and relationship.

I find doing this very useful to concentrate my mind on focusing on the things I want in my life and imagining how my life will look like.

I also imagine seeing myself in a position to be ready to buy a property on one of the lovely streets I walk by on my walks and visualise myself living there one day. This will also help to inspire you to work harder during the day on achieving your goals.

There is something magical about writing down your goals. The important part is to set a goal, so you have something to aim for.

So, set a goal and write it down and when you've achieved that goal, think of another goal and then write that goal down, and of course take action to achieve that goal by thinking of the steps you need to take to achieve your goal.

What does your ideal life look like?

If You Believe You Can Do It, You're Right

Become a self-fulfilling prophecy whereby you believe it will happen. Your mind works in ways to bring into physical reality the things you think about most of the time.

Most of us will never realise our true potential, so if you believe in yourself you can achieve what others think is impossible.

So, with more effort and concentration, the rewards will be worth it. You aren't going to accomplish anything unless you believe you can and take steps to achieve it through action.

Create a habit for success by listening to yourself and ignoring those who want to see you fail.

When you set a goal, think of the time, effort and discipline that is required to achieve it.

You'll find that ambitious goals are within your reach.

To achieve any goal, you will need to sacrifice something in return for what you want to receive.

You'll need to give your time and talents before a return on your investment. It sometimes takes many years of hard work before you achieve "overnight success" in the eyes of others.

You'll know from your actions whether you are moving towards or away from your goal.

But where others see despair, you'll see hope.

Your Progress In Life Begins & Ends In Your Own Mind

Every great idea began in the mind of a great person. Then, with careful planning and taking action, it was transformed into reality.

Continue to learn, grow, adapt and embrace change throughout your life to practise discipline and follow through on your good ideas.

The most brilliant ideas are only a dream unless you take action.

Write your goals down.

Only 3% of adults write down their goals and these people achieve five to ten times more than those who do not write down exactly what they want in life.

1. Decide: what you want?
2. Write it down on paper.
3. Set deadlines for your goal.
4. List everything you need to do to achieve your goal.
5. Make a plan from your list.
6. Take action right now.
7. Do something every day to move you closer to your goal.

Review your goals daily, ideally in the morning, and take action on your most important task first to accomplish your most important goal that you are working on now.

What are your most important relationship or family goals right now?

What are your most important career or business goals right now?

What are your most important financial goals right now?

What are your most important health goals right now?

What are your most important personal development goals right now?

What are your concerns or problems right now?

You should always aim to perform at the very best of your ability at work so that you can get the most done to benefit from the rewards from your career.

There is something magical in writing down your goals on a piece of paper with a pen. Start off by writing down your goal and put a date when you want to achieve it, so you have something to aim for. When you have achieved that goal write down another goal.

10 Steps To Achieve Your Goals

Review the list below every day to help you to achieve your goals.

1. Believe
You must absolutely believe that you can transform your life. Everything started as a thought so make your thoughts turn into a reality.

2. Visualise
Know what you want for your life and focus on making it happen.

3. Write it down
This is the key to your success.

4. Purpose
Know your 'Why' you want to achieve your goals.

5. Commit
Commit to making it happen.

6. Stay Focused
Stay focused to manifest your goals and do this daily.

7. Action Plan
Know what you want by writing down a list of tasks to achieve your goals.

8. Do It Now
Think of something that you can do now to show commitment towards your goals, even if you do a little thing every day towards your goals that will help you and get you closer to your dreams.

9. Be Accountable
Tell friends and family about your goals and seek outside help (like finding a mentor).

10. Review
Review each day to make sure you are on track because sometimes life gets in the way, so it's important to follow this list to see if you are on track.

Do these steps daily and you are on your way to achieving your goals.

"Write down your dream for it to become a goal.
Then break it down into steps to create a plan.
Then take action to make your dreams become
reality." — Laurence Lameche

 Awaken Your Inner Hero Within 24 Hours

1. Set weekly, monthly and yearly goals.
2. When you exercise, walk around your local neighbourhood, or when you are going to work or at lunchtime, constantly think about your goals and what you want to achieve in life.
3. Act with courage and boldness in the pursuit of your goals by taking action.
4. Every great idea has begun in the mind.
5. Write down your goals on a piece of paper with a pen.
6. Use the 10-step plan every day to help you to achieve your goals.

Live Each Day As If It Were A New Beginning

"Today will soon be the next day, that concerned you the day before."
— Laurence Lameche

SECRET #21 to Awaken Your Inner Hero Within 24 Hours

Live today as if it were a new beginning. Forget yesterday's setbacks, and ignore tomorrow's problems. Commit to making today the best day of the year. Imagine yourself at the end of your life in a rocking chair looking back on your life and thinking to yourself, *"I wish I could turn back time and do things differently with my life."* Today is your day, make it count!

Live today and every day as if it were your first day: a brand new beginning. And when you lay in bed, rest, knowing you've done your best.

What could you do differently today? Would you spend time in nature, or enjoying the simple pleasures of life, and spending quality time with your family, friends and growing business relationships? Every thought and moment spent will be precious.

Put past mistakes behind you and start afresh as if there was no past and only a bright new future. Well, today is in fact a new opportunity for a fresh start, so don't let it pass you by.

Misused Time

Every day, all of us have the same twenty-four hours available. Most of us on average spend eight hours working and eight hours sleeping. What you decide to do with the remaining eight hours you have left will have a big influence on the level of success you have in your life.

At the end of every day ask yourself this question, *"Have I given 100% of my talent and time today?"* If I owned this company would I be happy with an employee like me?

Have you done your best to meet the standards required by yourself to earn your pay so that you can sleep well at night?

Regardless of what the rest of the world is doing, create your own philosophy of success so it becomes like a habit that you do every day.

Life Is Short

So, make the most of it now and become who you were born to be. None of us know when our time here will end, so make every day count. Live life on your terms and live the life of your dreams today. Don't wait for tomorrow.

Be Young At Heart

Smile and laugh and don't take yourself too seriously. Life is short so why not make the most of it and have fun in every moment and situation and laugh at yourself and at life.

"Don't be afraid of dying, be afraid of never having lived." — Laurence Lameche

 Awaken Your Inner Hero Within 24 Hours

1. Live today and every day as if it were a new beginning.
2. We all have 24 hours in the day, so make sure that every minute counts during the day in being productive and that you are working on your life's purpose.
3. Life is short, so don't put off for tomorrow what can be done today.

Accountability

"Make things happen instead of waiting for things to happen." – Laurence Lameche

SECRET #22 to Awaken Your Inner Hero Within 24 Hours

Find other like-minded people who you can connect with, so that you are able to help each other on a regularly weekly or monthly basis to hold each other to account on achieving your goals each time you speak together. Think of what you want to commit to before your next call and write it down. This should help to inspire you to achieve the things that you have agreed to do before your next call and it gives you an extra push of motivation, because you won't want to speak to them if you haven't done anything meaningful.

Find someone to be your accountability partner, on ideally a weekly basis or a monthly basis. You could choose, for example, four people and speak to each one once a month arranged on the 1st, 2nd, 3rd and 4th week every month. You may need to go through a few accountability partners to find the right one for you, but it will be worth it.

You also may want to consider getting more than one accountability partner because sometimes, for many different reasons, it may not work out with them. You may want to set up agreements before you enter into choosing the right accountability partner for you – like arrange a certain day and time each week and commit to each other to make sure you make it on time on that day.

So, every week you can talk about the previous week's success or what you can improve on or do better next week and what your next week's goals are.

Who You Surround Yourself With Is Who You Become

The simple law of human nature says that if you want to have financial success, then surround yourself with other people who are financially successful. The same is also true with many other things in life. So if you want to be an entrepreneur, socialise with other entrepreneurs who have started their own companies. You want to get in shape... Get the idea?

All you have to do is to replace the things that you want to eliminate from your life, with habits that will benefit you to live to your true potential. So, take out the old bad habits and replace them with the new empowering ideas and habits you read about in this book that serve you better. This will help you to take one step at a time in your journey to greatness. Same amount of time but different results.

I am grateful for you spending your time with me; I know that people have busy lives with the many choices to make. So, I am proud that you have come this far on our journey together through these pages and I know that you are serious with wanting change. It is not about becoming an overnight success or getting lucky or taking some kind of shortcut.

You can start to incorporate these habits in your life and I want this book to be the turbo-charge you need to light the rocket that can take you to where you want to go in life. And what will fuel the rocket are your thoughts, actions and intentions – so get ready for take-off!

It doesn't matter where you are in life right now, whether you have these things or not: a relationship, family, good job, wealth and happiness.

There is a story that you must either stop telling yourself, or adjust, because it's stopping you from leading the life you desire in the areas that matter most to you. So, change your story to change your life.

Ask successful people these questions:

"How did you become successful?"

"What are the biggest challenges you've had in your life or career right now?"

"What advice would you give your younger self?"

"Sometimes the past hurts, but if you learn from it
you become stronger."
— Laurence Lameche

 Awaken Your Inner Hero Within 24 Hours

1. Find an accountability partner and commit to each other that you will speak over the phone or by video conferencing on a regular basis to set weekly or monthly goals that get you closer to achieving your dreams in life.

2. Remember: who you surround yourself with, you become.

Mentor

"A mentor is someone who holds your hand every step of the way through their easy, proven and transferable process."
— Laurence Lameche

SECRET #23 to Awaken Your Inner Hero Within 24 Hours

A mentor is someone who has already done what it is that you want to do successfully. Learn from their failures and successes, saving you the many years of trial and error having to figure this all out by yourself. All successful people in history have had mentors to guide them, help them and advise them on how to do things better through their wisdom, knowledge and expertise. Invest in yourself and find a mentor today who can help you take your life to a new level.

Find a mentor, someone that is already doing what it is that you want to do and learn from them, which could save you the 10, 20 or 30+ years having to figure this out all by yourself.

But choose a mentor carefully and make sure that they are credible as there are many out there that teach theory and haven't done what they are teaching you, so be careful. I only teach you what I do, not what someone else does and that's why my students succeed.

I teach you live in real time, under pressure while being videoed, to show you the step-by-step process that actually works and you can see other students just like you succeeding in real time. You've got to ask yourself a question: who else does that?

To succeed in the world today requires continuous learning, so lifetime learning in your field to stay current in this fast-paced world will keep you ahead of your colleagues and competitors. If your students believe in you, and what you teach works, then you are the greatest mentor in the world for person that understands you, believes in you and accepts you and follows your guidance – but you cannot be their friend, you need to be their mentor. They need to invest in you, otherwise they will not take it seriously. If they are not invested in you, then you are just a friend to them.

The only people on this planet I listen to are the people that have done what it is that I want to do and have done it well. You need to have someone who you can model and learn from.

Tony Robbins currently charges $1,000,000 for a twenty-minute phone call, once a month for 10 months of the year.

I have several mentors who I pay to help me in my life in all different areas and I will be sharing them with you in my 'Inner Hero Circle'. It has taken me a lifetime to search the planet to find these very special mentors and I have listed them below:

1. 'Life-Changing Manifestor' who gives you the secrets behind the scenes to transform your life.

2. 'My Book Coach' to help transform your ideas into your very own book and turn it into an Amazon No.1 Bestseller.

3. 'The Hollywood Insider' who will help you to become a master communicator.

Bonus

- Private Facebook Group Page to help you.

www.Facebook.com/Groups/AwakenYourInnerHeroWithin24Hours

Check out the mentor you want to learn from to make sure that they have actually achieved what it is that you want to achieve in life.

Make sure that they have a 100% money-back guarantee to protect yourself and also pay by credit card which will protect you further in case you need to get your money back because you are protected by your credit card company.

Invest In Yourself

When it comes to life, I believe that if we stop learning, we start to die. If you want to have more time, freedom, money and happiness in your life then never stop investing in yourself.

If you want to transform your life's experiences, then you'll need to gain more knowledge to have more wisdom which will give you more guidance and insight to go to the next level. Every year, I spend money to invest in myself on continued learning – by reading more books, audios, taking online training, courses and attending live events, to searching for mentors who can help me in different areas of my life. But make sure that you are learning from someone who is an expert in their field of knowledge.

"Some people stumble and lose their way in life and all they need is a helping hand."
— Laurence Lameche

 Awaken Your Inner Hero Within 24 Hours

1. Find a mentor who has already successfully done what it is that you want to do.
2. Invest in yourself and your continued education.

Action

"Action doesn't guarantee happiness; but with no action there will be no happiness."
– Laurence Lameche

SECRET #24 to Awaken Your Inner Hero Within 24 Hours

Reward yourself for the long hours or for every task you complete that brings you one step closer to your goal. It could be treating yourself by doing something you enjoy, eating something, watching a movie, spending time with your family or going out with your friends. Remember rewarding yourself is important to continue to motivate yourself to succeed.

If you want to change your future take action now.

A well thought-out plan backed up by action to create opportunities will lead you to success.

If you fail to act upon your dreams, the road will lead to failure. Because talk is cheap and action is all that matters.

Many people think that they want success, but as they do not back this thought up with drive, persistence and action, they will not get there.

Learn The Secrets From Other Successful People

Observe the actions of successful people to find out what principles they regularly use in their lives so you can copy this formula for success. The secrets of success can be learned by anyone who is willing to take

the time to learn, study and apply them.

You can learn from most people and you don't need to know them personally as there are many leaders in history that are no longer alive. So, study their lives and apply their principles that you learn to your own life to achieve greatness.

Set Deadlines

Become an effective person by creating a sense of urgency. Set deadlines and force yourself to priorities even if your activities don't require them. It will amaze you how much you can accomplish in a short amount of time.

Developing a habit of action may be challenging at first, but with practice the easier it becomes.

You'll Not Finish If You Don't Start

You may know people who looked back on their life and said *"if only I had done things differently ... if only I would have taken that opportunity when it came along."* These timid souls only have regrets to look back on what might have been, *"if onlys"*, and when they realised it, their life was almost over.

When I have a big decision to make, I ask myself this question, *"When I am very old, near the end of my life in my rocking chair, would I look back on my life and regret not making this decision today?"* I would then weigh up the pros and cons to making that decision and decide to either do it or not.

Life is filled with great success and failure at times. So, you have to make the most of the opportunities that come along during your lifetime.

It's up to you my friend to seize each day to take advantage of the opportunities that present themselves to you.

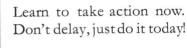

Learn to take action now. Don't delay, just do it today!

Imagine that this is your rocking chair, you got to ask yourself the question: "Will I regret this decision that I am about to make today, to either follow my dreams or to imagine what my life could have been?"

Motivate Yourself Into Taking Action

How you talk to yourself will determine your emotions whether they are positive or negative. What determines how you feel is not what happens to you but how you interpret things that are happening to you. Your version of the events will determine whether the events motivate or demotivate you.

To keep yourself motivated, you have to become an optimist to all words, actions, and reactions to the people and situations you find yourself in.

Although this may be challenging at times, you must refuse to let setbacks affect your mood or emotions in your daily life.

If you take action towards your intentions and vision of where you want to go, you will be far less distracted with emails and phone calls and other things sent to stress you and overwhelm you. Because there is more opportunity in the world now than at any other time in history to get ahead in life.

However, you must have a map to guide you to your destination, so you can get to the next level of life.

Once you have a crystal-clear vision, you will not let things annoy you or get you down that maybe once did as they will no longer have any power over you from achieving your goal.

I write this without possibly ever having met you, but I know that you have great potential because every person can make small shifts in her or his life that could potentially lead to great success. This question is whether you will realise your true potential.

High achievers believe in their vision and themselves. They practise and work hard to get the results they want rather than wishing something magical could happen for them but doing nothing about it.

The same is true for anyone who created abundance and wealth in their lives; they succeeded because they rolled up their sleeves and got to work on taking the right actions to realise their dreams. And they continued even when they were faced with obstacles.

The difference between those who think about success and those who go out and achieve it, is that the habits taught in this book don't work unless you do! Be willing to go the extra mile to get what you want.

You can achieve everything you want and desire, but don't give in to the naysayers. It's not going to happen by just hoping – so go out and do it.

As powerful as the habits in this book are to help you become the best version of yourself you can be, they won't change the quality of your life, your income or make you a millionaire unless you actually do use them.

You can't plan to use them or think about implementing them at some point in the future.

You have to put them into practice now and do them regularly by taking action today to realise your true potential.

"The power of belief is to believe."
– Laurence Lameche

Awaken Your Inner Hero Within 24 Hours

1. Take action today to create the future you want tomorrow.
2. Study other successful people to find out their secrets to success.
3. Set deadlines to create urgency.
4. Start at once whether you think you are ready or not.
5. Take action today on your most important task and get it completed immediately.

Conclusion:
Putting Everything Together

The key to great success, happiness, inner peace and awakening your inner hero within is for you to continue to learn and grow in life to be the very best version of yourself that you can be every day.

These skills are learnable through practice and when you develop the right habits in your life the world is your oyster.

Here are the 24 great ways that you can apply what you have learnt into your life right now. Feel free to review these principles over time so that you will remember them and they become an important part of your life in your thinking, actions and habits so that you can become what you were born to be and awaken your inner hero from within.

Secret #1   **Gratitude**: Practise being grateful every day and focus your thoughts on good things to attract more blessings into your life.

Secret #2   **Affirmations:** Listen to affirmations daily and create a list of your favourite ones to remind yourself during the day that 'You Can Do this'.

Secret #3   **Read:** Continuous learning is the key to improving any area of your life so read every day to grow and improve your skills.

Secret #4	**Listen to Motivational Talks and Watch Videos**: Regularly listen to motivational speakers to inspire you to reach new heights and to allow your mind to absorb this information that anything is possible and to think to yourself, *"If they can do it, so can I."*
Secret #5	**No Social Media When You Wake Up In the Morning**: Within the first hour of waking up, stop yourself from looking at social media and do something different. Turn off the notifications, alerts and put your phone on silent when you are working.
Secret #6	**Turn Off The News To Make You Smarter**: Turn off the negative news and you eliminate a lot of negativity in your life. There is nothing good about watching, reading or listening to the news that brings any benefit to your life, so switch it off and allow your mind to relax from the chaos of the outside world constantly bombarding your mind with negativity.
Secret #7	**Don't Let Other People Affect Your Mood**: Stay calm in frustrating situations and keep control of your emotions. Remember that no one can upset you unless you allow them to.
Secret #8	**Happiness**: Do things that make you happy. Smile to live longer and laugh at yourself. Find work that you love to

do – after all, we work for most of our lives so why not do something you love.

Secret #9   **Procrastination**: Because you can't do everything, learn to put off low-value tasks and only work on doing what the most important task is and do it now. Manage your time and discipline yourself to do the most important task first.

Secret #10   **Focus**: Work on one task at a time until it is 100% complete. Repeat to yourself, "Focus, Focus, Focus" when you are losing concentration. Plan your day in advance and value your time.

Secret #11   **Regrets**: Life is short and as each year goes by don't look back on what could have been. Instead, think about the possibilities that lay before you and what you can do now. Learn from mistakes and move on.

Secret #12   **Positive Mental Attitude**: You are in control of your thoughts, so be mindful of what you think about most of the time. Be positive and learn from experiences and situations that happen to you. Have an abundant attitude to life to attract more good things into your life.

Secret #13   **Knowledge**: The more you can learn

and apply that knowledge, the more abundant your life will be. Make sure you are getting the right advice because bad advice could end up costing you.

Secret #14 **See The Good In Every Situation**: Focus on your strengths and see the good in every situation that you go through in life. It is here to test us to make you stronger if you learn from the lessons.

Secret #15 **Thoughts – Be Careful What You Think**: Thoughts become things so focus on the good thoughts and eliminate the bad thoughts when they come up. You are in control of your mind, so fill your mind with greatness. Constantly repeat to yourself, "I can do it."

Secret #16 **Use Your Mind Wisely**: Read, study, think and plan for 30 minutes each day and also constantly review your goals.

Secret #17 **Working For Yourself**: Sometimes you have to make sacrifices when working on your dreams. There is always an answer to every problem.

Secret #18 **Change Of Direction**: Life can take you in many different directions so learn to adapt and change.

Secret #19 **Forgiveness**: There are many benefits for you to forgive, you can heal disease, live longer and it benefits your own well-being and inner peace.

Secret #20   **Goals**: Set regular goals and deadlines and work every day on doing something that will help you achieve them – see them like stepping stones to greatness.

Secret #21   **Live Each Day As If It Were A New Beginning:** We all have 24 hours each day, so make the most of every day because life is an incredible gift. Live each day as if it were a fresh start to a new beginning.

Secret #22   **Accountability**: Search for someone who can be your accountability partner and commit to regularly speaking to each other on a weekly or monthly basis to set goals and not to chitchat on less important things. Make this time together count so you can both be inspired by what each other is doing.

Secret #23   **Mentor**: Choose a mentor who can help you succeed in doing what you want to do. Invest in yourself and in your continued education as this could be one of the best investments you ever make.

Secret #24   **Action**: Motivate yourself to become your own cheerleader and look for the good in all situations. Be optimistic and look for solutions rather than problems.

Practise these principles every day so they become habits.

Use the principles in this book to become the best version of yourself possible. You are special and you have greatness within you. What a wonderful time to be alive.

If you liked this book,
please give it a 5-star review on Amazon.

Or recommend the book to someone you care about,
because it could help change their life. And it would
mean a lot to me if you could post about this book
on social media to let the world know that there is an
inner hero within them waiting to be found.

As a Special Thank You for doing this for me here is
a FREE Gift Video I made for you called *"I AM"*
Affirmations for Abundance in Health, Wealth, Success &
Happiness (For A New You!). Click on this link now:
https://tinyurl.com/yysx3qxa

Your Referrals Help Children's Wishes come true!
Help Us Help The Kids. We are giving back to those
in need when you refer a friend or family member that
buys this book, you're helping a sick child's wish come
true because for every book sold a portion of that will
be donated to **Make A Wish Foundation.**

About The Author

Laurence Lameche is an international No.1 best-selling author of *"How I Bought 3 London Properties For A Football Ticket"*.

If I can do it, so can you! My hope in writing this book is that you too can see your greatness within and live life on your own terms where money is rolling in and freedom is rolling out. I was born in London, England, but grew up in the countryside and I was raised in a single-parent family with financial hardships.

I went to multiple schools where I struggled and didn't get any qualifications which led me to the school of hard knocks! I have always had inner belief that I could achieve anything I set my mind to and that the only limits I have are the ones in my mind.

The one asset I do have is determination for a better life and this helped me to move to London and sleep in my car when I was 20 years old until I saved up enough money to rent a bedsit. Then, I went on to start my first business in the nightclub industry in London. After this, I figured out a way to acquire property for £1 without the need of a mortgage or a deposit and I wrote a book about it. Now, I teach online courses for different strategies in real estate.

None of this would have been possible without my greatest gift, my past. Even though I was bullied at school, have insecurity issues, I am quite a shy person, I am an introvert by nature and I prefer my own company, I know how to function by getting out of my own way.

I have created many easy-to-follow systems whereby I hold your hand every step of the way through my proven and transferable processes and techniques that allow people to live life to their full potential.

You need to spend time every day on developing you because it will change your life forever.

Even though we may never meet, I believe in you because you were born for a reason to achieve greatness in this lifetime and to awaken your inner hero from within. You have the power, now use it for your greater good!

Acknowledgements

The person I would most like to thank for writing this book is me, because if it wasn't for me this book wouldn't have ever got written. And I also want to thank you for buying the book and for reading it – congratulations for getting this far.

We reach our full potential in life by overcoming our inner villain to awaken our hero from within by gaining knowledge and information through experience, failure and success. Then, implementing what we learn by taking action and excluding everything that doesn't work, through trial and error. This way, we gain wisdom and we reach our full potential by being greater than who we were.

I thank you from the bottom of my heart.

Guaranteed To Change Your Life
or I Will Pay You $1000 in CASH!

This offer has never been done before in the history of publishing by any other author. But I believe so much that this book will help change your life, that I wanted to create an offer so unbelievable it would encourage you to buy the book.

The **"$1,000 Guarantee"** is ONLY offered if you bought this book yourself and was not given it as a gift. Laurence's promise to you is that you have to implement all the steps inside the book along with our terms and conditions listed here to qualify. Because if somehow your life isn't changed when you took action on what you learnt, he'll pay you **$1000 as his gift!**

Just make the moves and submit a "Proof of Action Form" which will activate this 100% risk-free $1,000 Money Back Guarantee. No one else has ever made such a guarantee like this before, except for Laurence Lameche. There's no way you can lose! I wrote this book to inspire you to take action with what you have learnt to help make a difference in your life.

You must read this book on the same day it is delivered to you by Amazon and you need to email us proof of this delivery on the same day it was delivered to you.

For the first video you record within 24 hours of reading the book, I would like to hear why you bought this book or if it was a gift, who gave it to you and where are you in your life right now and what do you hope for in this book that will make a difference for you in your life? What has also been your 3 most important takeaways from this book? Also within 24 hours record a video of yourself and post it onto your own social media pages like Facebook, Instagram and LinkedIn talking about your thoughts regarding this book while also holding the book when you are talking to the camera or you can always post a photo of the book along with your comments. This will help us to make a difference in the lives of many people that you care about by 'Awakening Their Inner Hero Within' make sure to use hashtag #AwakenYourinnerHeroWithin24Hours

On the 2nd day after the book has been delivered to you. Every day when you wake up in the morning video record yourself on your phone talking about what you learnt from today's chapter. Go through each chapter one day at a time by reading the tasks at the end of each chapter and say how this will help you today and what you will be doing in your day. Record videos on your phone every day between 6am to 9am in the morning and also between 20:00pm to 22:00pm in the evening and then post your videos everyday continuously for 24 days in a row onto our Facebook Group Page during these times every day telling us what your plans are for the day and how your day went and what did you learn today so we can celebrate you and the progress that you are making every day which will inspire other people in the group to help support and encourage you on your journey to become the hero you were born to be.

In the evening video share with us how your day went, what challenges came up during the day and how the chapter you read today helped you in any way overcome what you experienced in your life and how it will help you in the future and were you able to implement what you learnt in the chapter to empower you during the day? Tell us what you learnt today and how it will make a difference in your life? Also write comments in detail explaining your videos on your posts.

Then build on the day before by re reading yesterday's action points and reading today's chapter in full and to implement all that you have learnt in the chapter and also the action points at the end of the chapter for each new day

Record one additional video each day between 7pm to 10pm to talk about how your life has changed each day as a direct result of reading this book and taking action every day on what you have learnt in today's chapter.

You need to email us every day with at least one question about the chapter you have read, starting on the 2nd day after reading the book for the next 24 days in a row. Emails to be sent to the following email address: **MentorMeLaurence@gmail.com**

Please help, support and encourage your fellow Hero's by only making positive and supporting comments on other members posts within the Private Facebook Group. Also find an accountability partner here to help support one another on your journey to success.
Ask for help from your peers inside the group. Be kind and thoughtful. Do not ever show disrespect to anyone because we

are all one family. Always look for the good in other people just like a Hero would. Don't abuse or harm each other in any way because this is a safe environment for all people and anyone who hurts someone else's progress will be permanently removed from this group forever. Remember that it is a privileged to be a part of this amazing group of like-minded people.

Also post once every 7 days on your own social media pages to share with your friends how this book is impacting your life with the actions that you are taking over the last 7 days (so 4 posts within the month) share your experience about this book to help others. Ask at least 3 people on your Facebook page to share this video on their pages, remember sharing is caring.

Private message at least 3 different people amongst your friends every day for 30 days in a row on Facebook to tell them what a difference this book has made in your life and that you wanted to share this great book with them! In your message include a photo of the book along with the Amazon link for this book.

Comment on other people's posts in our Private Facebook Group page every day for the first 30 days to encourage and support other Hero's on their journey.

Also we need to hear from you over the next 12 months to find out how your life has changed as a direct result of this book. So on the 1st day of every month post a video on our private Facebook group page for the next 11 months letting us know how life has changed for you and what you are doing differently now? What has improved, got better, what goals have you achieved as a direct result of the secrets you have read about in this book. Remember to reread the book regularly or listen to it again during the year and as the years go by continually practice what you have learnt to make it a habit in your life

Within 24 hours of reading this book email us the names of the 3 closest people in your life and if this book hasn't completely changed your life they will need to confirm via video that they haven't noticed any changes in you which you'll need to post on our Facebook group page. Because this book does change lives and your life will be changed too but only if you make the moves.

Remember that I am here to help you, support you and to

encourage you through the pages of this book and that is why I wrote it to help you in your life right now. I wanted to create something unique that would encourage you to take action by implementing the ideas inside this book.

So if you bought this book to try and take advantage of me or this guarantee in any way then please go away now! Why would you want to do that to someone who wants to help you? Because this is my life's work and this is how I support my family. My intention is to help people who are honest, with integrity and have the right intentions who are here to learn and to improve the quality of their lives and to help their family.

This book helps many people around the world and I may decide to remove this book at any time if people start to abuse this guarantee. And this will result in many people missing out on this opportunity which has taken me a lifetime to figure out by myself and to put it all together in the chapters to help you.

And if this happens then also Make A Wish Foundation will lose out on the potential income they would have received from the book sales. All because some people didn't play fair. So my lawyers/team are observing the progress that people are making.

All actions listed here and within each chapter of this book must be implemented to qualify for the Guarantee. Remember that you have to make all the moves because this guarantee is based on implementation and taking action. If you make every move your life will improve guaranteed.

We want to encourage you to pass if forward and buy 2 copies of this book and give them away to friends, family and people who you care about. I look forward to celebrating your success. Thank you for investing in your future and I am honoured that you chose to read this book to Awaken Your Inner Hero Within 24 Hours.

Private Facebook Group Page:
www.Facebook.com/Groups/AwakenYourInnerHeroWithin24Hours

Books and Online Training
by Laurence Lameche

You may be thinking: 'Is it Easy?' 'Does it work?' and 'Can I do it?' And the answer is "yes" to all those questions because all my trainings come with a 100% money-back guarantee.

How I Bought 3 London Properties For A Football Ticket: **www.PropertyBookSecrets.com**

How To Get Sold Out Tickets To Concerts & Sporting Events For Face Value or For Less Money & Sometimes For FREE:
www.TicketsOnDemand.live

How To Network Without Talking To People:
www.NetworkingSecretsOnline.com

How To Rent Your Property Without A Letting Agent:
www.PropertyRentalSecrets.co.uk

Awaken You're Inner Hero Within 24 Hours
www.InnerHeroSecrets.com

Real life case studies of people just like you going from zero to property hero within weeks:
www.ZeroToPropertyHero.com

Either invest in an online training or give your money away to the government. I make all my online trainings so simple for you to understand, it will be like I am holding your hand every step of the way through these easy, proven and transferable processes.

All my video trainings are recorded live where I teach you in real-time what I am showing you to do. Because I believe in teaching you practically, so nothing is theory. And it will help you to take back control in your life.

I teach the strategies in this book in more detail online. I also offer more information, advice and guidance for anyone wanting help on their property journey and support first-time investors to get started by helping them achieve their property goals.

Laurence can be contacted by email:
Success@ZeroToPropertyHero.com

Book Awards for
'How I Bought 3 London Properties For A Football Ticket'
by Laurence Lameche

Some of the many awards this book has won around the world.

Runner Up
Hollywood Book Festival
Business Category

Amazon No.1
Bestseller

Bronze Medal Winner
eLit Awards
How To Category

Finalist
The Wishing Shelf Awards
Books for Adults (non-fiction)

Honorable Mention
San Francisco Book Festival
Business/Technology

Honourable Mention
New York Book Festival
Business Category

Official Selection
New Apple E-Book Awards
Motivational Self Help Category

Honourable Mention
Paris Book Festival
General Non-Fiction Category

Honourable Mention
London Book Festival
General Non-Fiction Category

Most people are under the impression that they need capital, perfect credit, or at least a down payment to acquire their own property.

A Real-Life Book! No PDFs Here...

In the first half of the book, Laurence shares his humour-filled stories of **WHAT** lead to his success!

Then, the focus shifts to explaining the business of **HOW**!

- *How was he able to start his first business with nothing but an idea?...*
- *How did he go from being a tour guide to property investor in less than 5 years?...*

Laurence answers those questions and many more, all while providing **tangible** instructions and tons of **straightforward** advice...

It all begins with Laurence's 3-Step Process:

- **Structuring A Deal**
- **Customer Relationships**
- **Standing Out In The Market!**

Laurence gives readers worksheets, real-world financial breakdowns, and advice on personal matters other industry leaders don't take into account!

Are You Ready To Discover These 3 Secrets?

Secret #1 How To Structure A Deal From A to Z

Secret #2 How To Take A Customer-Focused View

Secret #3 How To Stand Out In A Crowded Market

Newspaper, Magazines and Radio Quotes about Laurence Lameche

Mail Online

"Property Tycoon"

The**Negotiator**

"His Example Will Inspire Other People"

PropertyInvestorTODAY

"Laurence Lameche Is An Entrepreneur"

"Rags To Riches Story Began"

 BuyAssociation

"Property Mogul"

FEMALE FIRST

"Winning Ticket To Success"

 **Ham&High** Property

"Owner Of A Successful London Property Business"

 share radio

"Property Magnet and Expert"

THE SUNDAY TIMES

"Landlord offered his London flat for free to homeless family for Christmas"

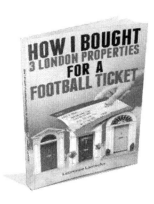

Buy A Copy of My Amazon
No.1 Best-Selling Book "How I Bought 3 London
Properties For A Football Ticket" Today

By Going To This Website Now:
www.PropertyBookSecrets.com

Tickets On Demand
by Laurence Lameche

Here is the secret way for you to buy tickets to sold-out concerts and sporting events at face value, less money and sometimes potentially for free. Here is my 3-step proven process.

1. **Research**
Things at home like:
- Venue
- Floor plan
- What to wear
- Price to pay
- Positive mindset
- Make a sign

2. **Action**
Getting to the venue:
- What time to get to the venue
- How do people get there
- Decide where to stand

3. **Result**
Getting the ticket
- Hold a sign, look at people
- How to avoid scalpers / ticket touts and never get scammed
- One simple negotiation tip

Getting The Ticket To A Sold-Out Concert Or Sporting Event, Every Time You Go, Creating Memories Which Are Priceless

If you would like to find out more about how you too can do this I have so far recorded 30+ live video trainings of me and other people just like you getting tickets at different events and locations, filming this over several years.

I have been doing this successfully now since 1998 all over the world and I have never had a single failure yet. Because of the overwhelming demand of people contacting me over the years and asking me if I could help them do the same, I have created the ultimate course to hold your hand every step of the way through this easy proven and transferrable process.

Go to my website to get immediate access now to all my 30+ live training videos.

As a bonus, you can download a free copy of my *Ticket Secrets* book.

For more information about my 3-step process to Research, Action and Result go to my website to get immediate access to all my training videos:

www.TicketsOnDemand.live

Networking Secrets
by Laurence Lameche

Would you like to learn my secret way of how to network without talking to anyone?

Every event I go to I take with me my business cards. Even if — like me — you're shy, an introvert or scared to network with people at these events, you must see it as a great opportunity to meet new people and to push out of your comfort zone.

I have come up with a quick way to network with lots of people and to collect as many business cards as possible without talking to people, and it works so well that sometimes the event organisers ask me to stop doing it. Can you imagine that!

Sometimes when I used to go to these events, I was normally stuck with the most boring person in the room, and they wouldn't ever shut up or go away.

I just couldn't ever think of a polite way to excuse myself from that situation to get away from them. I knew I'd be stuck with that person and I wouldn't be able to network or try to meet anyone else.

Also, I don't know if you are like me but I have always felt that whenever I went to these networking events or business events or conferences that I maybe would speak to the person sitting next to me if they talked to me first and then I would leave the event with one business card.

I would go home regretting that I wasn't brave enough

to collect more business cards and to go up to people to introduce myself. But I find it so painful to do that I would just rather leave.

So, for years I kept asking myself, "How can I network without having to talk to people?" And I finally discovered the Secret many years ago that allowed me to network without talking to people and the majority of people at the event come up to me and give their business cards to me without me asking them. It is truly amazing to see this live.

I have recorded many videos of different events I have been to over the years so you can see me do this in real time.

I even get my camera person to interview the people who see me do this and what made them want to come up to me and give me their business card and what they think of this idea – you'll be amazed by their reactions.

If you would like to learn more about this incredible way to 'Network Without Talking', I'll hold your hand every step of the way through this easy 3-step process that I have developed that anyone can do which will help you to network without talking to anyone as well.

Create the leads to motivate people to take action.

Convey your message in a way that's unforgettable.

Collect business cards with a simple, proven process that works every time for everyone, everywhere, building relationships that last a lifetime.

CREATE

Things at home like:

- Make a sign
- Take your business cards
- Take a clipboard, pen and sheets of paper
- Think about the venue you are going to
- What to wear
- Leave with a positive mindset

CONVEY

Your message at the venue:

- What time to get to the venue.
- How do people enter and leave the event?
- Decide where to stand.
- Hold a sign.
- Look at people.

COLLECT

The business cards:

- Learn how to communicate your message within seconds.
- How to quickly get rid of boring people.
- Use the 30-second rule to build a crowd of people waiting in line to meet you.
- This simple system works so well that sometimes event organisers and security may ask you to leave the venue (but don't worry I will teach you how to overcome this).
- The secret way to collect a lot of business cards and make new contacts and build future relationships so that people remember you, like you and want to do business with you.

A simple step-by-step process to networking and collecting business cards at every event you go to, creating relationships that last a lifetime.

I've even created the greatest business card in the world: it's a $1,000,000 Business Card!

You've got to network quickly with people and so try to talk to each person for 30 seconds to 1 minute – if they are interested in you, say, *"Let's catch up after the event, it was nice to meet you"* and move on to the next person.

Don't worry if you feel nervous or scared, because I always do! What I have learnt is to feel the fear and do it anyway!

As a bonus you can download a free copy of my *Networking Secrets* book.

For more information about my 3-step process to Create, Convey and Collect, go to my website to get immediate access to all my training videos:

www.NetworkingSecretsOnline.com

Property Rental Secrets
by Laurence Lameche

Each training module is a video course presented by Laurence Lameche to guide you through this simple step-by-step process to let your vacant property using only social media.

The Post

There is a very simple way to post your property on social media that will grab everyone's attention automatically.

The Where

I have a system for knowing exactly where your potential tenants will see your post.

The Offer

How to make your rental property a "no brainer" in the minds of those looking.

I took the knowledge I already had from renting my own properties over the last 20 years and was able to get a new tenant within 4 days!

Let's break it all down.

14 Training Video Modules

1. Facebook Advertising in Groups Pages

2. How I Rented My Property Within 4 Days on A Facebook Group Page

3. Facebook Profile Page Training and Secret To Getting People To Share

4. What Photos To Use To Advertise Your Property Online

5. How To Find Local Councils' Contact Details on Facebook and Google and How To Find Out What Councils Pay

6. 12k Facebook Views On A Video To Help A Homeless Family Rent A Flat For FREE At Christmas

7. Booking.com, HomeAway, Airbnb, Holiday Lettings, Gumtree Training

8. How To Contact Newspapers, Magazines, Radio

and Television. Plus: Where To Find Their Contact Details Online and How To Approach Them

9. The Secret To How I Got Into Newspapers, Magazines, Radio and TV Since I Was A Teenager

10. Ideas Of Who To Contact To Rent Your Property

11. £5000 (Gift) Lawyers Paperwork To Protect You

12. 2nd Part Of Training Of How To Evict A Holiday Guest

13. Phoning Hotels

14. How To Apply For A Mortgage Payment Holiday

- Private Facebook Group Page
- Bonus Training
- Lawyers Paperwork To Protect You
- Bonus Spreadsheets, Templates, Messages, Scripts and Emails

As a bonus, you can download a free copy of my Property Rental Secrets book.

For more information go to my website to get immediate access to all my training videos:

www.PropertyRentalSecrets.co.uk

Zero To Property Hero (Online Training)
by Laurence Lameche

If you would like to learn more about getting on the property ladder today Laurence created 'Zero To Property Hero' to help hold your hand every step of the way through this easy to learn proven process that you can learn about in the comfort of your own home.

What you will learn:

- 12 Training Modules recorded in real time with real students just like you with families like yours learning this process over 12 weeks via zoom.
- 50+ hours of property training showing students succeeding with my simple proven system that works every time for everyone, anywhere in the world.
- Replace your job within 3 to 6 months with property.
- Become financially free through property.
- Retire within 3 to 5 years.
- Learn how to overcome fear and control your mindset to succeed.
- Scripts to learn how to talk to property owners, landlords, estate agents, lettings

agents and watch Laurence do this live in the different modules.

- Learn many different creative strategies to get no money down property deals. No mortgage, no deposit, no job, bad credit and no experience and you will still learn how to do this from start to finish.
- Learn how to do Rent2Rent deals and Rent2SA deals renting landlords properties as serviced accommodation on Airbnb and potentially doubling the normal rental income every month.
- Become the only logical choice when it comes to property investing in your area.
- Save the 10 to 20 year learning curve that I went through all the trial and error, the pain and frustration so you don't have to figure all this out by yourself.
- You'll not only learn from my successes but also from my failures as well so you won't have to make the same mistakes.
- Find your accountability partner
- Join a private online community to get lifetime support
- Question & Answers each month for 12 months
- Case studies of students going through this online training

Who's this training for?

- Experienced and novice property investors. There are insights and "golden nugget" techniques found only here!
- All those with the desire to create passive income, to increase their property portfolio, or to move from one deal to the other
- Those who simply want to let one property for an extended period of time with no mortgage, and gain equity at the end.
- People who are fed-up and frustrated with property investing programs that haven't delivered on their promises.
- Anyone that wants to retire early, and live life on their own terms!
- If you're willing to discover all the possibilities available outside traditional property financing and exchange, then this training is for you!

Watch my free webinar now and invest in your future today? Get started on your dreams:

www.ZeroToPropertyHero.com

We also offer three other packages to suit all budgets depending on what level of training and support you need.

Silver Package

For our Silver package our leading trainers will help you to succeed on a weekly basis with one hour group training calls for our students where we hold your hand by helping you find property deals in the area that you want to invest in over the next 12 weeks (3 months) speaking to you and the other members every week helping everyone by making the phone calls for you to the landlords, property owners and agents showing you exactly what you need to say to get a yes and then negotiate the deal for you from start to finish helping you to succeed.

We also listen to you making phone calls yourself to practice and then we give you feedback on how well you did and what you can do next time to improve.

+ Standard package included as a bonus
+ Weekly Q&A's for one hour
+ Join our Zero To Property Hero room in Clubhouse every week and ask any questions you may have.

Gold Package

For our Gold package you will be working with our leading trainer helping you each succeed on a zoom call in a small group of 4 people for one hour per week for 12 weeks, where we will hold your hand by helping you find property deals in the area that you want to invest in. We will make the calls for you by speaking to the Property Owners, Landlords, Estate Agents and Letting Agents and we will also help you to negotiate the no money down deals for purchase lease options, Rent2Rents and Rent2SA's.

We offer a Success Guarantee (one property deal) within the next 12 weeks or our team will continue to help and support you every week for another 9 months so 12 months of weekly live coaching calls.
+ Standard package included as a bonus
+ Weekly Q&A's for one hour
+ Learning how to get Rent2Rent deals without paying a guaranteed rent or a deposit
+ We will give you video testimonials of several landlords that you can use as credibility to help you get more property deals
+ Join our Zero To Property Hero room in Clubhouse where you can listen to our leading trainers making live phone calls for our students on the Gold packages in Clubhouse to Landlords and Property Owners during week days every Monday to Thursday helping to succeed and answering any questions you may have.

Platinum Package

If you want to personally work with Laurence Lameche so that he can potentially help you become financially free within 12 months. By finding property deals in the area that you want to invest in over the next 12 months speaking to you via a private zoom call for one hour every week.

Laurence will make the phone calls for you on a weekly basis and to also listen to you making phone calls yourself to practice and then we give you feedback on how well you did and what you can do next time to improve.

Helping to personally hold your hand every step of the way showing you exactly what you need to say to get a yes and then negotiate the deal for you from start to finish helping you to succeed every week.

We offer you a Success Guarantee that you will earn £10,000 per month within just 12 months or we will continue to help you for another 12 months until you achieve your goals.

+ Standard package included as a bonus

+ Weekly Q&A's for one hour

+ Learning how to get Rent2Rent deals without paying a guaranteed rent or a deposit

+ How to kick out a tenant within 24 hours

+ Learn how to get around the 90-day rule in London for Serviced Accommodation

+ We will give you video testimonials of several landlords that you can use as credibility to help you get more property deals

+ Join our Zero To Property Hero room in Clubhouse where you can listen to our leading trainers making live phone calls for our students on the Gold packages in Clubhouse to Landlords and Property Owners during week days every Monday to Thursday helping to succeed and answering any questions you may have.

Our packages start from as little as a cup of coffee a day.

If you would like to find out more on how we can help you in your property journey then book a free 30 minute strategy call with us using this link and we can help you get started

https://calendly.com/mentormelaurence/30min

Awaken Your Inner Hero Within (Online Training)
by Laurence Lameche

Wake Up to Take Control of Your Life Today!

Awaken Your Inner Hero Within 24 Hours online video training modules will help guide you to a better life, to help move you towards personal change. It will act as a driving force for your success.

Learn how you can take back immediate control of your Time, Mind, Emotions and Financial Destiny! Make your dreams come true today. Where I'll hold your hand every step of the way through this easy, proven and transferable process that works every time for everyone who wants to awaken their inner hero within.

Everyone from Men, Women, Teenagers and Children from all walks of life who understand and apply these simple principles will benefit from the wisdom. Because you'll learn the Secret that **"They"** Don't **Want You** To **Know** About!

You may experience a **Changed Life** if you embrace this philosophy so **Be Prepared!** It will help you to uncover the hidden truth for a better way to live your life with Freedom, Abundance, Happiness,

Peace of Mind, Positive Attitude and Taking Action to Achieve your Goals. Remember Your Future Needs You!

You'll learn how to overcome your inner villain to awaken your inner hero to help you transform your life right now by applying the teachings.

Use positive thinking to change your attitude by making small changes to replace old habits for new ones and learn how to do it. Discover how to deal with criticism to not let people effect your mood.

Find a job you love or work for yourself and make success happen with ideas, motivation, inspiration and turn regrets into opportunity. Go from failure to success, anger to happiness, stress to peace, depression to sensational, negative to positive, procrastination to action.

Invest In Your Future Today:
www.InnerHeroSecrets.com

THE **BEST**

Free Gift

That Will Change Your Life Forever!

Learn how to claim your $497 worth of Inner Hero Secrets Mastery Information Absolutely FREE.

Including a FREE 'Test Drive' of Insiders' Inner Circle Superhero Secrets Membership

Claim Your Inner Hero Secrets Bonus – Go Here Now **www.InnerHeroSecrets.com/freegift**